Feng Shui Symbols

Feng Shui Symbols

A User's Handbook

Christine M. Bradler
Joachim Alfred P. Scheiner

illustrated by Klaus Holitzka

Sterling Publishing Co., Inc.
New York

Library of Congress Cataloging-in-Publication Data

Bradler, Christine M.
    [Feng Shui Symbole des Ostens. English]
    Feng shui symbols : a user's handbook / Christine M. Bradler, Joachim
Alfred P. Scheiner ; illustrated by Klaus Holitzka
        p. cm.
    Includes index .
    ISBN 0-8069-7153-3
        1. Feng shui. I. Scheiner, Joachim Alfred P. II. Bradler, Christine
M. Feng Shui Symbole des Westens. English. III. Title.

    BF1779.F4 .B7313 2001
    133.3'337--dc21

                                            2001042624

10 9 8 7 6 5 4 3 2 1

Published by Sterling Publishing Company, Inc.
387 Park Avenue South, New York, N.Y. 10016

First published in Germany under the titles *Feng Shui Symbole des Ostens* and
Feng Shui Symbole des Westens and ©1999 by Schirner Verlag, Darmstadt,
Germany
English translation ©2001 by Sterling Publishing Co., Inc.
Distributed in Canada by Sterling Publishing
c/o Canadian Manda Group, One Atlantic Avenue, Suite 105
Toronto, Ontario, Canada M6K 3E7
Distributed in Great Britain and Europe by Cassell PLC
Wellington House, 125 Strand, London WC2R 0BB, England
Distributed in Australia by Capricorn Link (Australia) Pty. Ltd.
P.O. Box 704, Windsor, NSW 2756 Australia

Sterling ISBN 0-8069-7153-3

Preface

Feng shui is the ancient Chinese art of creating harmony in living spaces. When applied to today's modern needs, such harmony requires the maximum use of every available feng shui remedy. Although these remedies and symbols originated in China, they are not entirely foreign to our culture. Animals such as dragons, turtles, and cranes and objects such as mirrors, crystals, helixes, and chalices are powerful symbols in Western culture as well. For the energies of these symbols to be effective, they have to be in the right place, which means that we must first become aware of their energies and then learn how to use them according to feng shui principles. The how-to necessary to do this is provided in this book. The symbols are alphabetically listed and include the classical Eastern and the more modern Western symbols. They are meant to be signposts for the reader who wants to choose the proper ones and place them in their optimal locations at home or at work.

About the Authors

Christine M. Bradler, originally a movement therapist, expanded her education by studying astrology, psychology, and dream therapy, with an emphasis on creative symbolism. This led her to study feng shui, to integrate its principles into her own life, and to found, together with Joachim Alfred P. Scheiner, The Creative Feng Shui Institute in Rosenheim, Germany. Convinced of the effectiveness of feng shui, she switched gears and made this art form the center of her life and efforts, even opening a feng shui store. She leads feng shui seminars, where readings and aura cleansing have become effective and valuable tools.

Joachim Alfred P. Scheiner, after receiving an M.A. in technical engineering, turned to Eastern philosophy and discovered the art of feng shui. He became convinced of its effectiveness, studied under Roger Green, William Spear, and Derek Walters, and became a feng shui practitioner himself. He is the co-founder of the Creative Feng Shui Institute in Rosenheim, Germany. His life is guided by the principles of feng shui. He is involved in several different feng shui related activities: he is the owner of a wholesale business of feng shui related products, a researcher and developer of feng shui remedies, a feng shui consultant, and a leader of feng shui seminars all over the world. His emphasis is on making people aware of their circumstances in life, how to find the appropriate feng shui symbols, and how to use them most effectively as remedies.

Contents

Introduction

Feng shui is the ancient art of creating living spaces that are in harmony with the universe. This art—a combination of folklore, religion, and science—is not confined to China and the Far East. It has been practiced in the West for some time. More and more homes and businesses are being planned and furnished according to the principles of feng shui, because it is not only the outside world but also our immediate environment that influences our physical and emotional well-being.

Feng shui is based on the Chinese philosophy of Taoism. When viewed separately from Taoist principles, feng shui seems to be simply a collection of odd rituals and practices. However, we find the Tao in everything—it is the absolute, the unity, which knows no beginning or end and is the source of all that exists. Tao created heaven and earth. Feng shui practitioners and people using it believe that the energy of the universe is present and flows through everything.

Lao-tse expressed it best: Tao is real and can be proven, even though it is passive and without form. It can be conveyed but not acquired. It exists in itself and by itself. It was before heaven and earth and will be for infinity. It gave the gods godliness and the world its being.

Chi, the vital energy of Tao, connects and activates everything and brings forth everything, and everything returns to it. Tao is like a huge ocean consisting of the waters of *chi.* This ocean is a constant movement of two currents: yin *chi* and yang *chi.* They are responsible for the waves, currents, eddies, and whorls, creating a Tao of ceaseless, flowing, and never-ending motion.

Feng shui means "wind and water" and is a kind of shorthand for the flowing and never-ending movement of Tao that finds expression in the natural order of the world. Feng shui is based on the conviction that everything is infused with life: trees, mountains, each stone and rock, every human being, earth and heaven. Everything is related to everything else. Everything in feng shui is dedicated to bringing about or reestablishing harmony in these relationships.

To achieve this, feng shui looks to astrology and astronomy for clues. Feng shui practitioners examine how a landscape influences a human being and try to determine how the elements, colors, and the four corners of the compass influence a person's life and fate.

The principles of Taoism are the hallmark of feng shui. Taoism believes that human patterns are only a mirror of the sacred order of the universe and that everything on earth is a mirror of heaven. That is the reason why feng shui has assigned a primary role to the planets and stars, the moon and the sun. The firmament is considered the first textbook of a feng shui consultant. Knowing how to decipher the secrets of heaven and earth is believed to be the key to influencing the destiny of nations and peoples.

Chi's central energy and life force is all around us. Freely flowing chi means harmony; interrupted *chi* means chaos. Feng shui is a method that removes disturbances and reestablishes the harmony between a person, the cosmos, and the Tao.

Wind and water (feng shui) influence the interaction of *chi* with the energies of nature. Peaceful harmony between all elements of heaven and earth is essential. According to feng shui belief, we can either be fatalistic and accept our fate or we can take life into our own hands and make changes. We can take actions that influence the harmony around us and thereby positively influence and improve our lives. We ought to see ourselves as a microcosm of the universe, as part of nature. Feng shui teaches us to live in harmony with ourselves and nature.

In this sense, feng shui is more than a popular trend in Tao living. It is a complex art that should not be reduced to simple rules, because unless we understand the principles behind

Taoism, feng shui is difficult to apply. It is a reverent system that provides practical advice about how to connect to the energies of the universe. It attempts to dissolve the barriers between the everyday and the sacred. Feng shui is a tool that allows us to become a conscious part of the cosmos, making it possible to grow beyond ourselves and reestablish harmony in our lives.

But what is harmony or good fortune? Taoist principles of feng shui tell us that good fortune means living a sacred life. Wholeness is rooted in nature, a nature that unifies human beings with the earth and the universe. To experience well-being or wholeness, human beings have always tried to be close to nature by surrounding themselves with its symbols.

Feng shui shows us which symbols can be used by anyone, for any situation or any surrounding. They are always adjusted to individual needs in order to create harmony and wholeness and to promote healing.

Symbols work on several different levels. One level in particular, while not always easy to comprehend or freely accessible to us, represents the very foundation of feng shui. It keeps alive our awareness of what we need in order to be whole, in tune with the universe, and connected to the Tao, the absolute. It makes us aware, consciously or unconsciously, that something is keeping us from being whole. It is the driving force behind our need for change.

Another level is the emotional one, where the energy of the symbols vibrate in tandem with our innermost needs. The more mindful we become, the more focused is the way that we use the symbols, and the more effective their energy will be for us and our environment.

Basic form of a Tibetan mandala.

The Ba Gua

The ba gua is a very effective and simple feng shui tool. It is a grid or compass used to analyze the layout of a building or an area. It represents the eight vital areas based on the eight trigrams of the *I Ching (Book of Changes).* According to ancient Chinese beliefs, this system contains all essential building blocks of the universe, from which all life flows. All cosmic qualities, objects, and elements can be described and analyzed by the eight trigrams.

The arrangement of the ba gua areas corresponds to the eight trigrams of the *I Ching,* creating a direct connection between the trigram and the vital areas (the ba gua areas) of human life. A ba gua compass makes a precise analysis of individual rooms of the home—or of any other area—possible, providing a wealth of insight and making it possible to draw conclusions about lifestyle and quality of life. The goal of feng shui is to create a balance between the different ba gua areas and thereby bring harmony, peace, and health to your life.

One of the most widely used ba gua systems is the Tibetan three-door ba gua. As the name implies, the starting point is a door. It may be a gate through which you enter a garden, an entrance door into the house, or a door entering a room. The entrance door is the opening through which energy enters a home, and is often referred to as the "gate of *chi.*" This makes it particularly important, if a house has several entrances or a room has several doors, to determine which is the main entrance.

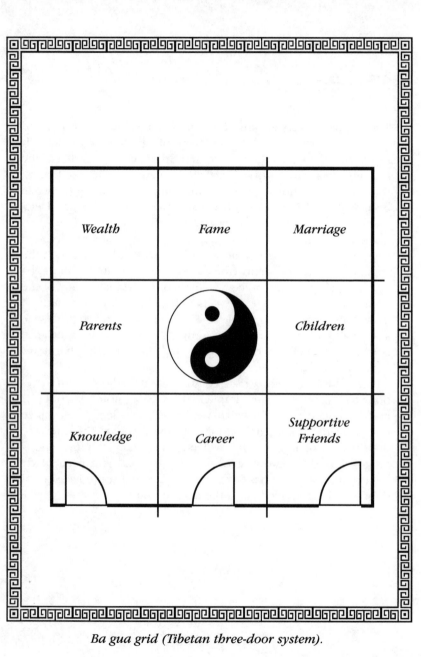

Ba gua grid (Tibetan three-door system).

Transferring the Ba Gua to a Room

To transfer the ba gua grid to a building or room, it is necessary to mentally divide the space under consideration into nine equal sections or squares. Draw a sketch on paper of the room or building and divide the length with two horizontal lines and the width with 2 vertical lines to make a grid system. The results are nine areas of equal size in which each box represents one-ninth of the total area (see diagram). The center square is considered the *tai chi*—the center—representing everything and nothing, and it is not part of the eight vital ba gua areas.

When the ba gua grid is used, we see that the entrance is either in the Knowledge, Career, or the Supportive Friends area. The wall along which the door is located is considered the baseline from which the rest of the ba gua squares are determined. The ba gua grid can be used for any type of space: a piece of property, a room, a house, an apartment—even a desk.

A tip for using a ba gua grid: Hold the grid in front of you and stand in the doorway. Imagine that the room is divided into a grid of nine squares. The Wealth area will always be at the upper left square and the Marriage area at the upper right, for example. It does not matter if the entrance to the room is on the right side, left side, or in the middle.

Interpreting the Ba Gua Areas

Each area of the ba gua emits its own symbolic energy, as expressed in its particular trigram.

Career

Trigram:	Water *(K'an)*
Element:	Water
Colors:	Black, blue
Season:	Winter
Time of day:	Night
Organs:	Kidney, bladder

This area is connected to the feng shui element Water. Because of its intimate connection to the ocean, the source of life, it is very powerful.

Water mirrors the ups and downs of life, as a brook meanders through the landscape.

The Career square shows us what we want to achieve in personal as well as professional terms. This area should be comfortable and orderly, allowing energy to flow freely. Disorder—with objects like shoes, pocketbooks, and cartons, etc. lying about, particularly in the area close to the entrance—will obstruct and hinder progress.

If this area is missing in the layout, the occupant will have difficulty finding the right path in life and professional goals will be difficult to achieve.

Resources:
- Aquarium • small indoor fountain • bowl of water • mirror
- wavy pattern on the walls or floor • waterfall poster • vase
- fish • indoor pond

Knowledge

Trigram:	Mountain *(Ken)*
Element:	Earth
Colors:	Yellow, brown, beige
Season:	Early spring
Time of day:	Early morning
Organs:	Spleen and stomach

Like a rock at the edge of the ocean, the Knowledge area symbolizes stability and safety, because it is connected to the element Earth (one of the 5 elements of feng shui). Contemplation, learning, and wisdom is the theme in this area.

This area mirrors our inner wisdom, self-knowledge, and what can be accomplished through our own efforts. It represents a strong but passive energy.

This is an ideal area for meditation or a private library. It is a good place for study and reflection—to collect one's thoughts. This area should be furnished sparsely and should not be too dynamic.

If this area is missing in the basic floor plan, it means that the occupant will continue to make the same mistakes over and over again because being reflective is difficult.

Resources:
• Books • pictures of mountains • unicorn sculpture • candle • crystal lamp • yin/yang symbol • mandala • minerals or semi-precious stones • Buddha statue • elephant sculpture • Kuan Yin • crane • vase • mobile • parasol

Parents	Trigram:	Thunder *(Chen)*
(Family)	Element:	Wood
	Colors:	Light green (jade)
	Season:	Spring
	Time of day:	Morning sunrise
	Organs:	Liver and gall bladder

The Parents area not only refers to our biological parents, but also to people that have shaped and still influence our lives: mentors, teachers, supervisors, bosses, and people of authority or high position.

While this area is an open and accessible energy, it is also influenced by our past. This is the area of the order of nature, symbolized by thunder. We are reminded of how important it is to look to our roots and to build on that strength.

If the area is missing in the floor plan, the possibility of family tension and health problems is very real.

Resources:
• Dolphin sculpture • healthy, strong plants • flowers • indoor pond • aquarium • DNA double helix • wind chime • dragon • bamboo plant • peach • mobile • trigram band • elephant • thunderbolt • swastika • stag • crane

Wealth

	Trigram:	Wind *(Sun)*
	Element:	Wood
	Colors:	Green
	Season:	Early summer
	Time of day:	Before noon
	Organs:	Liver and gall bladder

This energy is very strong, like the wind. It belongs to the feng shui element Wood. It strongly influences the flow of energy.

The Wealth area mirrors not only financial prosperity, but also good fortune and blessings. It is the place of lucky circumstances—often called "coincidences"—that are helpful for getting ahead in life.

The word "wealth" not only refers to material things such as money, but also to inner wealth (joy, optimism, satisfaction), which is much more precious than is often thought.

If this area is missing in the basic floor plan, it could mean possible financial difficulties caused by thoughtless actions.

Resources:
• Aquarium • indoor pond • strong plants • bamboo plant • golden fruit • waterfall poster • DNA double helix • fountain • two-duck sculpture • other objects showing two of something • mandala • orchids • rocks • stones

Fame	Trigram:	Fire *(Li)*
	Element:	Fire
	Colors:	Red, orange, violet
	Season:	Summer
	Time of day:	Noon
	Organs:	Heart, small intestine

The word *fame* (or *honor*) often is misunderstood. It refers not only to external images, recognition, and honor from the outside world or how well people think of you. It also refers to the inner light, to being aware, to self-respect, and to self-knowledge.

The Fame area belongs to the feng shui element Fire, and its energy supports passions, talents, and intellectual abilities.

The Fame area is opposite the Career area, indicating that the journey of life, after all, has a goal. This area encourages us to think of how we can give meaning to our lives.

If this area is missing, the occupant might have a tendency to pay too much attention to the opinions of others, to have too little self-confidence, and to feel unappreciated.

Resources:
• Diplomas or trophies • bright lights • Buddha statue • candles
• crystal lamps • DNA double helix • crystals • butterfly mobile
• peach

Marriage (Relationships)

Trigram:	Earth *(K'un)*
Element:	Earth
Colors:	Yellow, brown, beige
Season:	Late summer
Time of day:	Afternoon
Organs:	Spleen and stomach

Like Mother Earth, the Marriage area contains the most powerful female principles: integrity, receptivity, and kindness. It is a highly nurturing energy, sometimes too generous and too giving.

This area mirrors the full spectrum of relationships: friendship, marriage, platonic friendship, professional relationships, and business partnerships.

When creating this area, it is important to furnish it with symbols of solidarity, love, and receptivity. Try to avoid objects that express separation and loneliness.

When this area is missing in the layout of the room, it will be difficult—particularly for women—to create fulfilling relationships with their partners. Relationships with neighbors and colleagues often will be problematic.

Resources:
• Two-dolphin sculpture or pairs theme in other subjects • crystal lamp • minerals or semiprecious stones • red roses • DNA double helix • mandala • Buddha statue • peach

Children	Trigram:	Lake *(Tui)*
	Element:	Metal
▬▬ ▬▬	Colors:	White, silver, gray
▬▬▬▬	Season:	Fall
▬▬▬▬	Time of day:	Late afternoon
	Organs:	Lungs and colon

Like the depths of a lake, this energy is a mirror of our very core—
the depth of our feelings. Becoming aware of the potential that
this energy represents means that we can make full use of it and
make it work for us in the future.

The Children area is not only a mirror of our biological children,
but also is a symbol of the future and progress. All ideas that we
want to realize have their roots in this area. When pursuing plans
to open a business, for instance, the power of the energy in this
area should not be underestimated. This area is where joy and life
are born.

When arranging this area, give free rein to your imagination.
This is the place where creative shapes and colors will greatly
improve the flow of energy.

If the Children area is missing in the basic layout of the room,
its occupant might easily be prone to depression and melancholy,
money might be spent more on practical things than on hobbies,
and the relationships between parents and children are usually
very difficult.

Resources:
• Crystals • sculpture of playing dolphins • wind chimes
• fanciful pictures • mobiles • flowering plants • egg

Supportive	Trigram:	Heaven *(Chi'en)*
Friends	Element:	Metal
	Colors:	White, silver, gray
	Season:	Late fall
	Time of day:	Evening
	Organs:	Lungs and colon

The energy in the Supportive Friends area symbolizes heaven, masculine energy, authority, and leadership.

It represents all who stand by and support us: neighbors, friends, and charitable institutions—even our guardian angels. It includes all who, through their selfless actions and service, are a blessing in our lives. Older people can also be a great source of help when they pass on their experience to the younger generation.

If this area is missing, the occupant often feels helpless and alone in his struggles. His position in life and his health might be rather weak.

Resources:
• Crystals • dolphin group sculpture • DNA double helix • pictures or figurines of angels • bells • parasol • Kuan Yin statue

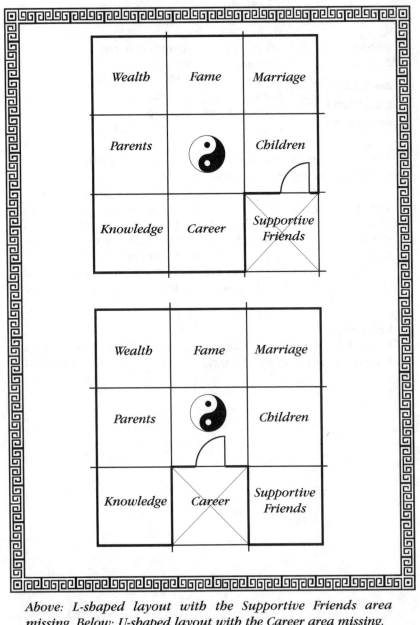

Above: L-shaped layout with the Supportive Friends area missing. Below: U-shaped layout with the Career area missing.

Using the Ba Gua Compass

It is important to keep in mind that in feng shui every thing and every form has to be in balance and complete, a requirement that is met in the case of a square or rectangular space or structure. Irregular and triangular shapes are considered detrimental and negative.

• L- or U-Shaped Layouts

When a space is unbalanced (L- or U-shaped), the existing layout must first be "expanded" to make it either a rectangle or a square. The expanded space added is considered the "missing area." If the energies of the missing area are not available to the occupants of the room or home, the people will be negatively affected in the long run, so it is essential to remedy such situations. This is done by strengthening the area with the appropriate symbols or resources, or "increasing" it with mirrors.

However, missing areas actually may be added or activated outside irregularly designed houses. For instance, if the length and width of an addition to a house (a porch or balcony) measure less than half of the length and width of the home, the addition will strengthen the house. Occupants of the home will benefit noticeably from the energy of the added area. A garden might also strengthen a "missing area."

After the layout of the house or room—on the paper plan—has been made square or rectangular, the new, now-harmonious shape is divided into nine equal squares and, depending on where the entrance is located, the eight ba gua areas are assigned.

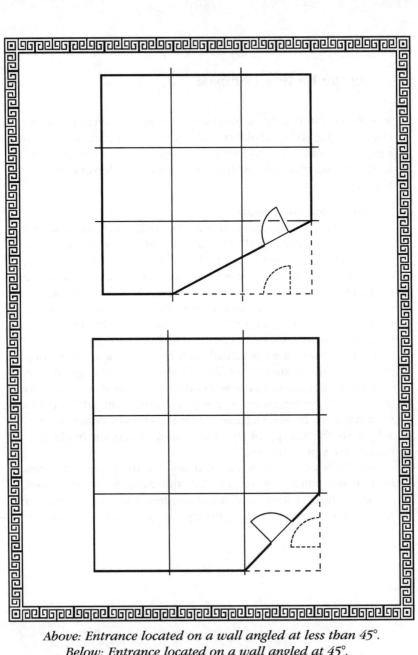

Above: Entrance located on a wall angled at less than 45°.
Below: Entrance located on a wall angled at 45°.

• Entrance on an Angled Wall

When an entrance door is located on an angled wall, the use of a ba gua compass might be more difficult. But here, too, the rules are relatively simple:

If the angle of the wall where the entrance is located is less than 45°, the wall—on paper—is simply "moved" straight (as shown in the top diagram, opposite page). If the wall angle is exactly 45°, the direction in which the door opens determines the direction in which the wall—on paper—is "moved," as shown in the lower diagram on the opposite page.

Make sure that you do not forget to mark the newfound area as the "missing area" on your plan.

• Balcony, Porch, and Terrace

Many basic layouts have missing areas, occupied by balconies or terraces. Don't make the mistake of counting these as part of the main house, because porches, balconies, and terraces are outside of the walls of the main buildings, and thereby are outside of our "bodies."

• Several Floors

If your house consists of several floors, you need to create a ba gua grid for each floor. The baseline always is the place from which you enter each floor. The entrance to each floor is usually the last step of the flight of stairs.

In an apartment building, the public staircase always is outside of your home and is not to be included in the ba gua plan. Start the grid at the entrance to the apartment.

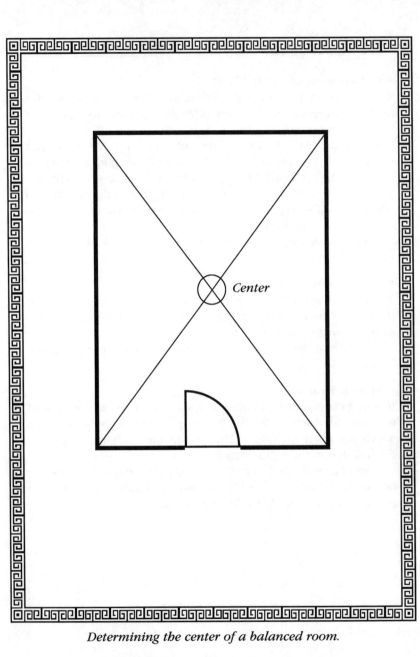

Determining the center of a balanced room.

The Center

The center of a room is considered the middle, the *tai chi*, from which we gather our strength. Whenever body and soul are centered, the greatest amount of strength and power will be available to us. Yin and yang are in harmony.

Each house and each room has its own center, just as your body does. As the ba gua compass shows, by dividing a space into nine equal sections we have created a center, which is called *tai chi*.

A house or a room also receives its energy from its center. If the center is disturbed, the occupants often experience instability and feel unsafe.

First let's see how the absolute center is determined. In a well-balanced floor plan, with, for example, a rectangular or square shape, it is relatively easy to determine the center: it is the point where two diagonals meet.

In case of an L- or U-shaped layout, the procedure is similar because the floor plan is "expanded" to create a balanced form. With irregularly shaped floor plans, things are more difficult. But here is a simple method to solve the problem: transfer the layout of the room or house, done to scale, to a piece of cardboard and cut it out of the cardboard. The middle—the balancing point—can be determined by balancing the cardboard on a large needle or nail. The place where the cardboard remains balanced on the tip of the needle represents the center, the *tai chi* of your home.

The center of every home and of every room should be free and unburdened so that the energy, the *chi*, can circulate freely. In old buildings, we often find that the center of a house, home, or room has been artfully emphasized, often with round or star-shaped mosaics built into the floor covering, or an artfully painted or sculptured structure on the ceiling. Frequently, there is an extraordinarily beautiful chandelier on the ceiling in the center. But a stairwell or an elevator in the center of the house or

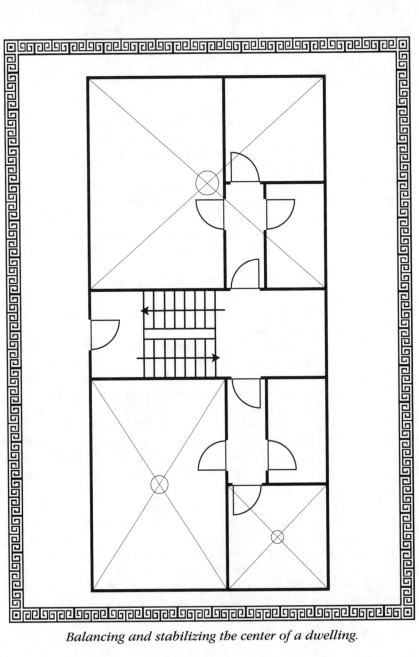

Balancing and stabilizing the center of a dwelling.

building creates a lot of strife and restlessness. A thick dividing wall, a chimney, or storeroom in the center of a house could indicate a lack of energy and a difficult life.

To rebalance such a situation, activate a substitute center between two rooms (for example, the living room and bedroom). Some suggested resources to do this are given in the Symbols section that follows.

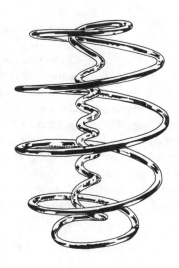

Affirmation for an entrance area.

Affirmations

The word *affirmation,* which has a Latin root, means *approval, confirmation, support.* Even in ancient times, people in every culture knew about the power and effectiveness of affirmations. Affirmations were carved, painted, chiseled, embroidered, and displayed above the entrances of many churches and homes, and often written simply in chalk above the front door. They appeared on everything, including stone tablets, wooden plaques, garlands—even pillows. Affirmations have been used as a matter of course in everyday life for a long, long time as blessings and remembrances, or for protection.

The choice of affirmation—a saying, verse, or poem—is up to you, but each affirmation should represent your innermost thoughts.

Applications:
• For protection above the entrance to an office or a child's room
• For reinforcing motivation
• To express gratitude.
There are many more uses. Let your creativity and imagination be your guide.

Ba Gua Areas:
• Any ba gua area will do, as long as you can clearly see and read the affirmation.

Example of an Affirmation:
May God protect and bless all who enter and leave this house.

Symbols

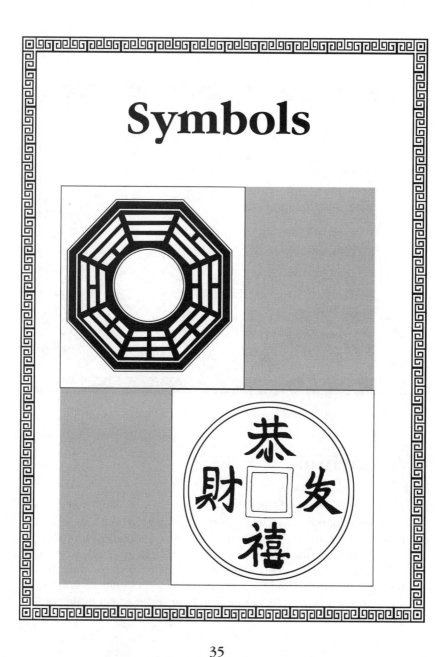

Wealth, abundance, fruitfulness.

Aquarium

An aquarium with fish, plants, and constantly moving water is a microcosm of the ocean. It contains everything that is powerful and creative about nature—its diversity and the possibility of growth.

If goldfish are used it is important to choose only eight red or golden specimens and one black. The black goldfish has the job of taking in and displacing the bad luck of the other eight. It is essential to replace a dead fish immediately in order to keep the equilibrium and, beyond that, to keep *your* well-being intact.

An aquarium is a classic feng shui remedy. In China, they are displayed in office buildings and restaurants, always in the appropriate ba gua area.

For a long time, people in Central China sacrificed the heads of fish to the god of wealth. To this day goldfish in an aquarium serve the same purpose, signifying: "May gold and precious stones fill this house." In Chinese, goldfish is written as *chin-yü,* a combination of the two words "gold" *(chin)* and "abundance" *(yü).* The goldfish therefore is a symbol of gold in abundance! A picture depicting two goldfish is also considered a symbol of fertility.

Applications:
- To increase and vitalize the energy in a room
- For relaxation and to relieve stress
- To strengthen the Water element of a person or a room.

Ba Gua Areas:
- Wealth
- Career

Important:
- Do not place the aquarium next to the toilet or bathtub, and never place it in the vicinity of an oven or chimney.
- The aquarium needs regular care. The water needs to be clean, clear, and fresh.

Affirmation:
I immerse myself in the collective spirit and feel protected. I know that I will receive what I need.

Angel

Virtue, spirituality, humility, composure, and the power of silence.

In the Old Testament, angels were the messengers of God's revelation. It was only later that Judaism, under Persian influence, introduced the concept of the heavenly hosts and God's heavenly household. The birth of Islam is said to have taken place when Allah ordered the Archangel Gabriel to bring his message, the Koran, to the prophet Mohammed (570–632 AD).

The earliest portrayal of an angel is in the Priscilla catacombs in Rome, dating from the first half of the 2nd century. Not until the 4th century were angels pictured with wings. In the 9th and 10th centuries, angels again did not have wings, but were represented by tall, dignified, boys or men in brilliant white robes—an expression of purity. The attributes assigned to angels also changed constantly. The lily at the Annunciation of Mary became the symbol of virginity; palm branches, a symbol of victory; musical instruments and incense burning, to praise God; trumpets, to announce the Last Judgment; various implements of suffering were a symbol of Christ's suffering, etc.

In the celestial hierarchy we find nine angel choirs (3 times the sacred number three): throne, cherubim, seraphim; rulers, principalities, power; archangel, angel, virtue. The cherubim represent a special embodiment of the Almighty—the protectors of the lost paradise and the guardians of the Ark of the Covenant.

The seraphim are primarily in charge of the duties of worship. The aristocrats among the angels are the archangels, who have names and specific functions. The highest among them is Michael, the warrior who defeated Satan. Many artworks are testament to this revered archangel. Raphael is primarily the protector and guide of the suffering. The archangel of peace is Gabriel. Uriel, the fourth archangel, appeared at the tomb of Christ. Depictions of celestial hierarchies are found most of all in Byzantine art and subsequently in Italy.

Philosophers described the relationship between people and angels. For example, Thomas Aquinas (1225–1274) said: "Man has not been promised less than being the equal of angels.... Man will become most like an angel to the extent to which he is able to learn about them.... The human spirit, liberated from earthly conditions, sees in the angel himself in an ideal state."

The countless opinions, writings, and works of art concerning these heavenly beings show us how prominent a place they occupy in the earthly life of people and how many great thinkers and artists throughout the ages have been captivated by them. In the end, angels are our connection to the sacred powers of the heavens, reminding us of what is within us and what we should strive for: virtue, spirituality, humility, composure, and the power of silence.

Application:
Using sculptures or pictures of angels is a way of asking for their protection and guidance.

Ba Gua Area:
• Supportive Friends

Affirmation:
I rely on the heavenly wisdom and guidance that is protecting me at all times, and I feel safe.

*Moon gate as entrance to the garden: symbol of
peaceful yin of the goddess of the moon.*

Archway or Gate

Although gates and archways are always an invitation to enter or
walk through, they also serve as barrier, protection, or obstacle in
the form of a garden gate, front entrance, temple gate, or

entrance to a city or grave site. They may be symbolic of the gates of heaven.

Archways and gates, crossings, and thresholds are places of transition between two areas, two worlds, inside and outside, the known and unknown, the here and the hereafter.

Gates and doors can be huge, decorated with many imaginative, symbolic details. Entrances to temples in Asia are often flanked by ferocious-looking figures, usually lions, allowing only the initiated to enter, sending away everything evil, such as demons.

In feng shui it is generally the house or apartment door or the garden gate that defines the transition from the public to the private—the outside to the inside. Any such structure should have a protective, solid appearance and be easy to open and close.

In a garden, a gate or archway can be used to separate the ornamental from the vegetable garden. Such archways are usually enhanced by climbing roses or other climbing plants or flowers. When the entrance to a property is wide and open, a large archway with climbing roses can serve symbolically as protection.

Applications:
• As a buffer between two areas
• As protection at an entrance
• As a support for climbing rosebushes in the garden.

Important:
• A gate or archway should have a solid and sturdy appearance.

Affirmation:
This gate offers entry and protection for me.

Protection.

Ba Gua Mirror

The ba gua mirror has a very special meaning in feng shui and is considered a powerful symbol of protection.

The ba gua mirror is octagonal with a convex or concave mirror in the center, surrounded by the eight trigrams. It should only be used outside and should be placed either above or next to the entrance. Make sure the mirror does not reflect neighboring buildings, an entrance to another's home, or trees, so as not to harm any of them.

Applications:
- A flat mirror to reflect possible harmful influences
- A convex mirror to diminish and scatter negative influences of walls and roof edges
- A concave mirror to distort images of oppressively large buildings, telephone lines and power lines and poles, or large trees.

Important:
Clean the mirror regularly to assure its effectiveness.

Affirmation:
I feel safe and protected.

Bamboo Plant

Humility and long life.

In China, the bamboo plant has always been one of the most useful natural products. The plant is a popular motif in Chinese calligraphy. It is considered the measure of all things. A famous Chinese tradition says that the artist must become a bamboo tree before he can paint one.

Bamboo derives its symbolism from its characteristics:

• Its trailing branches bow to the ground because its heart is empty. An empty heart is humble, which makes the bamboo tree a symbol of virtue.

• The tree is compared to a noble master, because it never changes. The tree stands upright and proud through every season and the worst storms, always convinced of its power. It is a symbol of trust and permanence.

• The tree is forever green and never changes. It is a symbol of long life.

• When set on fire, bamboo branches explode with a loud boom which, people believed, could drive away thunderstorms. Bamboo trees were also considered messengers of the gods. For a long time they were used for fireworks to greet the New Year and for other festivities, suggesting that at the conclusion calm and peace would return.

• Since the words for "bamboo" and "prayer" sound alike in Chinese, bamboo shoots are also used during prayer ceremonies. A vase with bamboo branches can be used to increase the effectiveness of the prayer.

• Bamboo, pine, and plum are the "three friends of the winter." Together they are the symbol of a long life.

• In feng shui, bamboo is the symbol of the element Wood and therefore of growth and prosperity.

When planting or bringing a bamboo plant into the house, provide enough fertilizer so that it can grow to its full splendor.

Applications:
• As a fast-growing evergreen plant, bamboo trees or plants are excellent for diminishing negative influences of sharp edges and corners coming from buildings that face the house

• Together with a pond (yin energy) in the garden, bamboo has good yang-balancing aspects

• Inside the home, a bamboo plant is very effective in softening corners, reducing the loss of energy through large windows, and providing needed support for Wood or Fire people.

Ba Gua Areas:
• Parents
• Wealth

Affirmation:
I am open to life, allowed to be curious and to grow.

Clarity and composure.

Bell

The bell is used in many cultures, partly as a musical instrument, partly as a mystical and ritual object. Its sound is used not only to call people together, but also to call supernatural powers. The latter use has made it a symbol of cults in many cultures.

In East Asia, a bell is struck on the outside with a pole or wooden clapper. Depending on its sound, a bell might announce good or bad news. The word in Chinese for *bell* sounds identical to that for "to pass a test" or "success," which has made it a favorite for playing word games.

Because of its shape, sound, and the material of which it is made, the bell is assigned to the feng shui element Metal, and is used as a symbol of clarity and composure in meditation.

Applications:
- As a ritual object, at the beginning of meditation
- As a symbol of protection, at the entrance or in the hallway
- To welcome friends (and angels).

Ba Gua Area:
- Supportive Friends

Protection.

Box Tree

In antiquity, box tree bushes or trees, together with cypress and yew trees, were often used to decorate cemeteries. They were considered to be the trees of the gods of the underworld and the Anatolian mother goddess Cybele. The wood of the box tree was a favorite for making boxes with elaborate carved figures of the gods. More recently, the wood was used for the mallets used by the Freemasons and in China, until the beginning of the 20th century, to make the characteristic belt weights (buckles).

The leatherlike leaves of the box tree remain green throughout the year. People in the Alps consider the tree a symbol of durability and love to use the branches—together with catkins—for Palm Sunday arrangements, which are blessed in church and then kept at home for the whole year. Since it is a very slow-growing tree, the box tree is also a symbol of longevity.

In Germany, farmers love to plant them on each side of the front door or in their gardens to keep evil spirits away. The branches are woven into wreaths as part of the tree of life and decorated with colorful eggs at Easter and with candles at Christmas. Trimmed into a cone or globe shape, the box tree can be found in many of the great gardens of castles and palaces.

Applications:
- As a guardian at the front door in a planter
- As a wreath at the entrance to the house or apartment
- As a garland above the front door.

Ba Gua Areas:
Depending its the shape, the plant can represent a specific element and can strengthen a specific ba gua area:
- Supportive Friends: tall trunk and ball shape
- Career: planted in undulating rows alongside a walkway

Path to enlightenment.

Buddha

Gautama Siddhartha renounced his royal status in order to live a life of meditation 2500 years ago. Sitting under a tree, he at last found the reason for all suffering and sorrow. Then he became the Buddha, and his teachings became a worldwide philosophy.

The life of Buddha, the Enlightened One, is the oldest example of how we can free ourselves from sorrow and guilt without divine intervention. Buddhism is one of the oldest teachings of redemption in the world, and to this day it has millions of followers. Buddhism is the path to self-enlightenment, serenity and peace—not by turning way from the world, but by making it possible to live in it. Buddha changed yoga exercises and meditation—which were part of an austere and world-renouncing lifestyle—into practical exercises meant to diminish the trials and tribulations of the everyday life.

Since Buddhism has become well known in the West, we, too, can use meditating Buddhas as symbols of enlightenment and absolute wisdom.

The various statues and pictures of Buddha that are available stand for different aspects on the road to enlightenment (such as practical wisdom, generosity, wholeness), and can be used accordingly.

Applications:
• For a meditation corner, altar, or room, as a symbol of inner wisdom and self-knowledge
• To support a goal and express the meaning of life.

Ba Gua Areas:
• Knowledge
• Fame

Affirmation:
I am connecting to the wisdom, wholeness, and peace within me.

Mortality and lightness of being.

Butterfly

In ancient Greece and Rome the butterfly—perhaps because of the many different stages it goes through in the course of its life—was the symbol of the eternal soul. The Greek goddess Psyche is usually depicted with butterfly wings.

Its lightness, characteristic also of elfin beings, dream images, and magical figures, which are often depicted with butterfly wings, could well be a reminder to us of the fleeting nature of joy, pleasure, and cherished moments. The butterfly might be the most perfect image of the lightness of being.

Many dream interpretations consider the butterfly to be the symbol of the metamorphosis that the dreamer needs to go through in order to find the essence of the dreamer's being.

Applications:
• As a mobile to activate the flow of *chi*
• As a silk butterfly to add to a bouquet
• As a wooden sculpture, with or without a magnet attaching it to a door, etc.

Ba Gua Area:
• Fame

Affirmation:
I am connecting with the lightness of being.

Sacred light or fire.

Candle

The candle is the symbol of light and fire. Candles have always been part of religious rituals: baptism, communion, weddings. At the altar, the candle is the spiritual light and expresses the connection to God.

The basis for the symbolic meaning of light in Christianity is the words of Jesus: "I am the light of the world." All Catholic churches maintain a perpetually burning candle, signifying an eternal light which is to intercede for the deceased, guiding them on their way home.

The rituals of praying in front of lit, sacred candles as a protection against storms, floods, lightning, and illness are deeply rooted in folklore. To this day, Catholics have a candle blessed in Church at the Mass of the Light on February 2.

Applications:
• To create a warm atmosphere for a get-together with family and friends
• To illuminate
• To focus meditation.

Ba Gua Areas:
• Fame
• Knowledge

Affirmation:
I acknowledge, trust, and connect to the light within me.

Chimes

Chimes are usually made of hollow or solid metal tubes with a clapper in the center of the group. The sound created should be clear, pure, and considered pleasant by the people living with them. Choose them with this in mind. Many different kinds of chimes are available. They may be tuned according to the scale or the planets.

Chimes are very important feng shui remedies. They can be used to slow down or guide the flow of energy, or to announce a person entering a room or home.

Chimes are effective even if they are motionless. Their effectiveness is based on their symbolic meaning.

Applications:

• Where there is a direct line between a door and a window, or a door and another door, to slow down and disperse the flow of energy

• At a window where external, detrimental influences exist (to soften sharp lines or edges of a house or roof, telephone pole, etc.)

• As a guard when a desk is placed so a person's back is to the door (see lower drawing on opposite page)

• To minimize the loss of energy in a sun room or winter garden

• To create distinct zones in a room that is used for two different activities (for instance a work area in a bedroom)

Warning and protection.

• As a door chime to welcome guests.

Ba Gua Areas:
• Works well in any area but particularly well in Parents, Children, and Supportive Friends areas

Affirmation:
There is a song in the room and I feel safe.

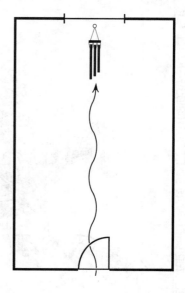

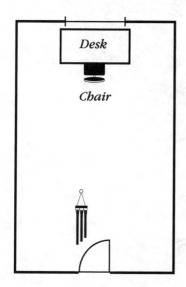

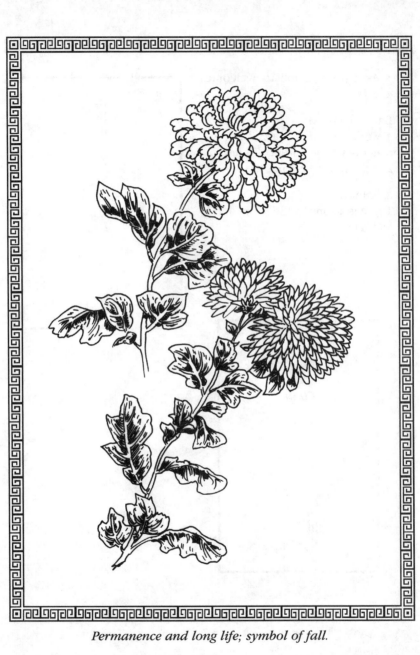

Permanence and long life; symbol of fall.

Chrysanthemum

From the huge variety of flowers and trees, Chinese scholars elevated four to be "the four noblest" or "the four exemplary ones." They are the plum, orchid, bamboo, and chrysanthemum. All are symbols of nobility and were considered by the educated elite, who knew how to write, as the four most favored flowers.

In East Asia, the chrysanthemum is a highly valued flower. In Japan it is part of the Emperor's emblem, and in China it is considered the symbol of fall, or the 9th month of the Chinese calendar. It is the symbol of permanence and long life. In China, rice wine from the previous year is treated with chrysanthemums. In pictures, the flower appears together with other symbols from nature. The pine tree and chrysanthemum are used together to express the wish: "May you have a long life."

The chrysanthemum, as the symbol of fall, is compared to a wise, educated person who lives a simple life and meets everybody with kindness—even those of ill will.

In the West, we grow not only the traditional white and yellow chrysanthemums that bloom in September and October, but also the smaller varieties as potted plants for indoors and in flower beds outside the whole summer. They are excellent indoors as an air filter, are easy to care for, and the blossoms last a long time.

Application:
• In the garden, on a balcony or terrace, or indoors. The flowers last a long time and are also excellent for flower arrangements. They bring great joy to all.

Ba Gua Areas:
• Because of the colors and shape, the classic chrysanthemum is assigned to the feng shui element Metal, making it a good choice for the Children and Helpful Friends areas.

Circle

The most important and widely used geometric symbol is the circle. It is considered a complete shape. A circle has no beginning and no end, no direction or orientation. In mystical tradition, the circle is the symbol of God, the ever-present center, complete and unassailable. This is the reason that the circle is the symbol of heaven and everything spiritual.

For several mystical cultures, circles are considered protection against evil spirits and used to be drawn around a person performing an exorcism. Nobody is allowed to step into the circle. Some feng shui disciplines enclose unfavorable numbers inside a circle in order to limit and neutralize their influence.

In astrology, a circle with a dot in the center is the symbol of the sun. In alchemy, the circle is the analogue for the metal gold. In Christianity, a halo is usually a perfect circle; concentric circles are a sign of creation, similar to those created on the surface of the water when a stone is thrown in the water. The Chinese yin/yang symbol expresses its duality in a circle. In Zen Buddhism, a circle means enlightenment.

Because of its shape, a connection is created to everything that approaches a circle. The circle acts as a balancing force when people try to solve problems. Decisions are made at a round table. Even in traffic designs, a circle is used to harmoniously connect several streets from different directions and allow traffic to flow smoothly.

In feng shui, the circle is assigned to the element Fire, like all other round shapes. It stands for heaven (yin) and for the human spirit. Round-shaped living spaces, while they unlock intellectual and spiritual pursuits, are less favored because they don't provide orientation and stability.

Applications:

• To divert negative influences, for instance if the house number is 4

• As a round rug for a narrow room, or in a hallway that has several doors (see floor plan at right)

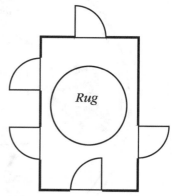

Rug

• In front of an entrance door, in the shape of a mandala or spiral

• In order to collect or attract cosmic energy (see drawing of circular pavement on opposite page)

• Round objects in a picture support the element Metal.

Ba Gua Areas:
• Children
• Supportive Friends

61

Chinese good luck coin.

Coins

Metal coins have been used in China since the 7th century BC. As is the case in many other cultures, in China coins are thought to bring good luck. Antique coins from China had a square hole in the center, through which the energy of the earth (yin) could enter. The round shape corresponds to the energy of the heavens (yang).

Special lucky coins had different symbols and signs on the surface. A bat means "Good luck is right in front of your eyes." Nine coins on a string signify uninterrupted good luck. Good luck coins were often worn for protection or to bring good luck. They were also thrown at the bride and groom during wedding ceremonies—the bride had to catch them with her skirt. Such bridal coins were minted with inscriptions, such as LONG LIFE, WEALTH, GREAT HONOR or MAY YOU GROW OLD IN HARMONY.

In feng shui, coins are also good luck or protection charms. Several coins (three, five, or nine) are strung on two red (the color signifying joy) silk ribbons. The ribbons are fed through the square holes in the coins' center and tied together to make a good luck ribbon, which is hung near the entrance to attract good luck and defend against harm and evil.

Applications:
- A large coin in a glass bowl lined with red or blue velvet
- 8 coins strung on a red silk ribbon hung near or above the cash register
- 5 coins as a good luck ribbon outside the entrance, hung either vertically or horizontally

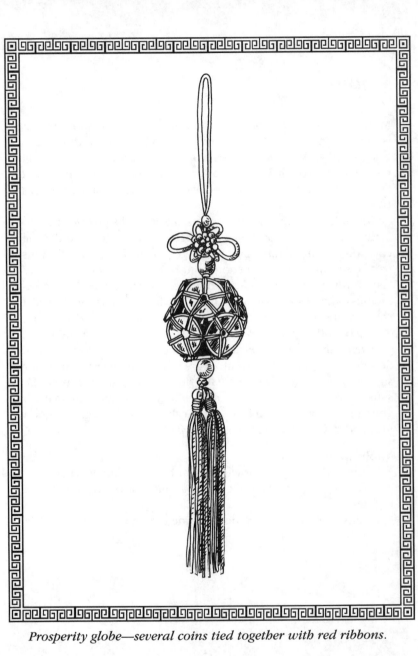

Prosperity globe—several coins tied together with red ribbons.

- 3 coins in a red envelope placed under a healthy, strong plant as a symbolic gesture of letting money grow
- 4 coins in a square red envelope attached to each bed leg, out of view, for continuing good luck.

Ba Gua Area:
- Wealth; in a room, on a desk, also on the sales counter

Affirmation:
Money is energy and I let it flow, giving and receiving.

Colors

Johann Wolfgang von Goethe was the founder the physiology of color, and his teachings made colors a subject of importance and worthy of study. For him, colors were a testament to a higher order.

Colors are a bridge between the here and the world beyond, simultaneously representing the connections that exist between body, spirit, time, and space. The sun is the originator of all colors, the source of life, and the reason why life exists. Nature is the coordinator of colors.

Goethe not only explored the nature of colors, but also studied their effects on the human psyche. He noted: "Experience has shown that individual colors can influence a person's mood and disposition."

This fact alone should challenge us to take advantage of the power of colors. The possibilities are endless, from tablecloths, curtains, and rugs to objects such as vases, bowls, flower arrangements, pictures, paintings, sculptures, lampshades, art objects (both store-bought and homemade), and plants. Different ways of painting the walls of a room and the different shades we have available to us today provide many creative possibilities, inside and outside of the home.

Feng shui provides guidelines on how to use colors according to the five feng shui elements and yin and yang, and gives information about the symbolism and dynamics of colors in general. A basic rule is that red and black should be used sparingly. Too much red creates aggressiveness and tension, and black can cause depression and pessimism. The way a room is used also determines the choice of colors; for instance, a bedroom or a place used for relaxation calls for quiet and gentle colors, while stronger, more joyful colors are more appropriate for living rooms and kitchens.

White

White is considered the most complete of all colors. It is difficult to find anything negative about it. In some cultures, however—as in China and for a long time in Europe—white represented death and grief. The belief remains that death precedes life or that life is part of death and each birth is, in a sense, rebirth.

The positive meaning of white is connected to the role it plays in initiation ceremonies. It is the color of innocence and virtue, of unbroken light, of absolute truth, victory, the ultimate transfiguration, and eternal glory. For many people white stands for wholeness, the ideal, and grace. Pure white in China, as in the West, is associated with virginity.

White neutralizes all other colors and is pure. Choosing white means that all possibilities are open, but it can also mean that a person who chooses white is unable to form an opinion.

In feng shui, white is the color assigned to west, to the feng shui element Metal, and stands for fall and evening. It is also a symbol of aging.

Attributes:
• White improves concentration and clear thinking.

Ba Gua Areas:
• Children
• Supportive Friends

Black

Generally speaking, black is the color of destruction, death, darkness, the night, and honor. Black represents grief without hope, in contrast to the messianic grief of white. Black means falling into nothingness with no chance of return. Black is also considered the color of letting go of conceit, vanity, worldly desires and things, and it is the color of humility. Some believe that black confronts us with our own personality.

The first emperor of China, after he defeated the red Chou Dynasty, chose black as the color for his dynasty. According to the control cycle of the five feng shui elements, the color black (Water) extinguishes the color red (Fire). It took 100 years to change back to red as the color representing a dynasty.

In feng shui, black is assigned to the north, to the feng shui element Water, and stands for winter, night, money, and wealth.

Attributes:
• Black is difficult to absorb and should be used as an accent color only (as borders, bowls, etc.).

Ba Gua Area:
• Career

Red

Red is a fascinating color and one of the earliest colors mentioned in almost every language. Its symbolism is based on two things: fire and blood. Red attracts attention and means power, energy, authority, and conquest. All emotions that make your blood boil, like love and hate, will bring the color red to mind.

Red is by far the most forceful color, calling attention to everything for which it is used. It is a masculine color and the opposite of the passive, gentle blue and the innocent white.

In ancient Rome, red was the color of admirals and aristocracy. Byzantine emperors wore red clothes exclusively as a symbol of power and wealth. In China, red was believed to be the color of life, which would keep evil powers away; it was therefore used for protection.

In very early graves in China, archeologists found cinnabar and red chalk placed in coffins in the hope that because of this gift they would remain in good favor with the deceased. As a symbol of life, luck, and joy, red is the color of the bride. Red is also a significant color on the Chinese stage. The actor with a red-painted face represents a holy person, and one of the three house gods—the one who is wearing a red robe—is the one who is the high-ranking and wealthy god.

Red and green are symbolic colors in Chinese paintings—both are the colors of life and vitality. They also mean healing and calm, because to get well or stay healthy you need quiet and serenity.

In feng shui, red is assigned to the south and the element Fire. It stands for summer and noon—it is also the symbol of youth.

Attributes:
• Red is activating and stimulating, improving assertiveness and dynamism. But red, like black, should be used as an accent color only.

Ba Gua Area:
• Fame

Green

Green fits somewhere in between blue, the color of heaven, and red. It mediates—calming and refreshing. The green shades of spring inspire hope and the fulfillment of dreams. Green stimulates imagination and empathy and gives wings to the soul.

Folklore, too, tells that green is the color of hope and life. It awakens curiosity and encourages exploration, because it is the source of vitality. It also calms the nervous system, lowers high blood pressure, strengthens will power, and contributes to tranquility and harmony. There are many different shades, and it is a good choice for rooms that should be restful. Green is also a good color for stimulating mental/intellectual activities. Neutral green colors call to mind vacations, forests, meadows, and recuperation.

In feng shui, green is assigned to the east, the element Wood, spring, and morning, and it is the symbol of growth and expansion.

Attributes:
- Green supports healing and stimulates creativity
- It facilitates clarity and a positive attitude to life.

Ba Gua Areas:
- Wealth
- Parents

Yellow

Yellow is the brightest, most intense, and most radiant of all colors—it is like sunshine. Goethe says that yellow is the color that is closest to the color of light. It is cheerful, lively, and gentle. People in need of a psychological boost should wear yellow.

Yellow also has a brightening effect, which makes it the ideal color for small rooms that receive little or no sunlight. Yellow uplifts the spirits and makes it seem as if the sun is shining, even on a cloudy and gray day. A brilliant lemon yellow has the strongest effect.

Yellow is also a color that makes people pay attention. In traffic signals and warning signals, yellow is part of everyday life in towns and cities.

Since the 6th century in China, yellow has been the color of honor and could only be worn by the emperor. Ordinary people were forbidden to wear yellow clothes for a long time. Yellow became the color of China for a very long time.

In feng shui, yellow is assigned to the center and the element Earth. It stands for late summer and afternoon. It is a very positive color and a symbol of long life.

Attributes:
• Yellow is balancing and calming
• It contributes to a feeling of safety and stability.

Ba Gua Areas:
• Marriage/Partnership
• Knowledge
• Center

Blue

Blue, one of the deepest and least physical colors, is the agent of truth, the color of translucent, compressed empty air, the color of crystals and diamonds. It is the color of the sky. Blue is the symbol of spirituality, harmony, friendship, care, faith, belief, sympathy, prudence, and compassion.

Blue is the coldest color. The shadows of sunlight appear to be blue. Vincent van Gogh painted trees blue when they stood in the shade. Ice and snow in sunlight have a blue shimmer, and skin

Blue, the color of crystals and diamonds.

turns blue when we are cold. It is not a color that says coziness and comfort.

In the battle between heaven and earth, blue and white fight red and green—as in the painting where St. George is fighting the dragon. Blue is also the color of the coat of Mother Mary.

Standing for intellect and spiritual insight, blue represents the positive side of imagination and utopian ideas.

In the past, indigo blue was the main color of clothes worn by ordinary people in the East.

For painting walls, it is best to stay with light blue tones, because they convey a sense of space and openness. Dark blue is an invitation for the occupants of the house to withdraw and become too isolated.

In feng shui, the color blue, like black, is assigned to the north, the element Water, and stands for winter and night.

Attributes:
• Light blue stimulates creativity and openness
• Deep blue colors subdue and create distance.

Ba Gua Area:
Career

Orange

Mixing yellow and red produces orange, an exciting but less intense color. It is a color that stimulates creativity in an exciting, dynamic way. It is not quite as hot as red, but reminds one of a fire glowing in the fireplace or a campfire. Orange is a social color and speaks of fun and good company.

Many adjectives are connected to this color: ripe, full, lively, warm, dry, cozy, autumnal, sociable, youthful, fresh, bright. Depending on the shade, orange is either assigned to the feng shui element Fire or to Earth.

Pink

Pink is the color of femininity, tenderness, beauty, and harmony. It is a weaker version of red and enriches white, mixing masculine and feminine energies. Pink also stands for innocence or the awakening of young love and romance. In China, pink is a favorite color for bedrooms to support a happy marriage.

Assigned to the feng shui element Earth, pink goes well with brown.

Violet/Purple

Violet is the color of thoughtfulness and calm, of careful thought through actions, of balance between spirit and mind, passion and intellect, but also of love and wisdom, since it consists of equal parts of red and blue.

In antiquity, purple was considered the most beautiful and aristocratic color during Holy Week. It is connected to the energies of completion. It is the color of high ideals, loyalty, truth, the powerful and well-to-do, and of people who are particularly lucky.

Both violet and purple are assigned to the feng shui element Fire.

Brown

From ocher all the way to a dark earth brown, this color and its many shades brings us back to earth. Brown also signifies positive interactions with Mother Earth and is the color of fall and sadness. In the early days of Catholicism, brown was the color of humility (*humilitas*—from *humus,* "earth") and material poverty, thus the brown habits of some of the mendicant orders.

All shades of brown are assigned to the element Earth.

Ba Gua Areas:
• Marriage
• Knowledge

Rejuvenation.

Crane

The crane is the messenger of spring and the symbol of rejuvenation. A crane's wing was used as an amulet against tiredness and exhaustion, because people admired it for untiring strength in flight.

In China, it is considered the symbol of long life and is often depicted together with the pine tree and a stone, to triple the symbol of longevity.

The crane is also the symbol of wisdom. Expressions like "heavenly as a crane," or "divine as a crane" point to this characteristic. A picture of a crane perched on a rock and looking at the sun symbolizes an important authority who can see everything. A crane flying towards the sun expresses the desire for social advancement.

Applications:
• As a metal sculpture in the garden
• As an image on a parasol, for a room decoration.

Ba Gua Areas:
• Parents (health)
• Knowledge

Maltese Cross

Ankh

Sun wheel

Latin Cross

Cross

The cross is not only a symbol of Christianity, but has forever been used for orientation: to distinguish between above and below, left and right. Its endpoints signify everything four-dimensional and represent the four directions of the compass.

A cross within a circle (the sun wheel) is not only meaningful in cosmology, but is also a symbol of the four seasons of the year. The vertical and horizontal lines of a cross divide a square into four equal parts. This scheme was often used in city designs.

In coats of arms we find several different versions of the cross: the Maltese Cross (or the Cross of the Order of St. John) with its four split arms; the swastika as a symbol of Buddha. The ancient Egyptian ankh was a symbol of life to come. The ankh was made of the cross in T form plus a circle, the symbol of eternity. In the last few years, the cross has been used more and more as an emblem by different esoteric fellowships. The

Latin Cross in Christianity is the original sign of sacrifice, but because of Christ's resurrection, it became a symbol of eternal life and the triumph over death.

Crosses are found not only in churches, but almost anywhere in daily life; as boundary markers, traffic signs, or window mullions. In the case of the latter it is important to remember that an uneven division of a windowpane or door negatively effects the energy in a room or space and its occupants. Any division should be symmetrical and harmonious.

Applications:
• At the entrance door, depending on the desired effects and as mullions or window lattices (see diagrams below)
• A sun wheel on the door as protection against negative influences.

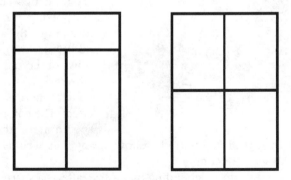

Balanced, symmetrical window lattices.

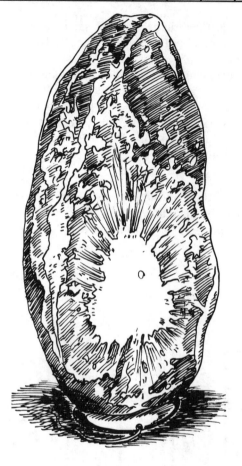

Crystal Lamp

Crystal lamps are made of rock crystals (transparent quartz crystals), which were formed more than 250 million years ago. Rock crystals are usually colorless, but may have reddish or yellowish tints, due to the presence of iron oxide, and are made up primarily of silicon dioxide.

When illuminated by candles or light bulbs, crystal lamps emit life-supporting negative ions into the air. In addition, the energy flow of crystal lamps vibrates to the right, which increases this effect. The colors of the spectrum of the light emitted by crystal lamps (red, yellow, orange, as well as white) also add a sense of comfort.

A rock crystal lamp, depending on its size, affects a space several meters (6 feet or more) wide, and twice that when the lamp is lit.

Many people today spend most of their time indoors (home, office, etc.), and the atmosphere inside buildings strongly influences our well-being. Scientific research has confirmed that vitally important negative ions are reduced indoors, due to the variety of electrical equipment we are surrounded by today (TV, radio, computers, mobile phones, etc). All of the above cause fatigue, lack of concentration, and depression, which, in turn, negatively affect productivity and psychological well-being.

Applications:
• To increase negative ions in the room and to have something pleasing to look at in the living room and bedroom
• To balance against too many positive ions (from technical equipment) in offices and workrooms
• To create a comfortable and life-sustaining atmosphere in medical or therapeutic offices
• To support the healing process in sickrooms
• To defend against left-flowing energies from TVs and computers.

Ba Gua Areas:
• Knowledge (yellow, orange, white)
• Marriage (yellow, orange, white)
• Fame (red)

Affirmation:
I am cleansing all surfaces of disruptive energies in order to remain or get well in body, mind, and spirit.

Vitality and protection.

Crystals

Crystals are very popular remedies in feng shui. They disseminate, scatter, guide, or activate energies almost anywhere in a room or home.

The quality of the crystal is important. Only flawless, faceted crystals made from high-quality material will be effective.

The facets of a crystal create a reflecting surface much like a small mirror, and therefore are ideal to influence the flow of energy. It is not by chance that crystal chandeliers were suspended from the ceiling in the entrance halls of palaces and castles in the past and are now popular in large homes.

The most popular are round (yin) and drop-shaped (yang). Ball-shaped crystals can be used in a room. For decorative purposes, they may also be star-, moon-, heart-, and octagon-shaped.

In addition, crystals have wonderful side effects: sunlight, when touching a crystal, turns into the eye-catching colors of the spectrum. This is the reason that prisms are also called rainbow crystals.

Applications:
• In a window in order to prevent loss of energy
• Between a door and a window, when the door and window face each other, to redirect the flow of energy
• In long hallways, to slow the flow of energy (see drawing on page 84)
• On corners or edges, to lessen their cutting effect (aggressive energy). See drawing on page 85.

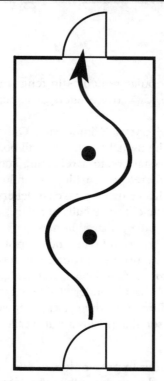

Crystals between two doorways.

- To activate energy in static rooms
- In small rooms, to keep energy flowing
- In the center of a room, to stabilize and focus energy
- In a window, to disperse negative energies (sharp edges, etc.)
- In a window, to energize a room with rainbow colors
- Between door and bed, to dissolve a potential conflict.

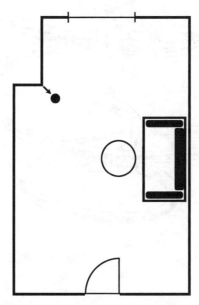

Ba Gua Areas:
• Everywhere, but particularly useful in areas for Children and Supportive Friends

Important:
• Crystals need to be cleaned on a regular basis to maintain their effectiveness. Dusty/dirty crystals produce and reflect dusty/dirty energy.
• The size of the crystal should be in proportion to the size of the window/room/hall, etc.

Affirmation:
The transformation of energy supports wholeness. May the messenger of light bring clarity and insight into my life.

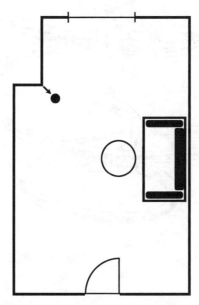

Crystals to lessen the effect of a sharp corner.

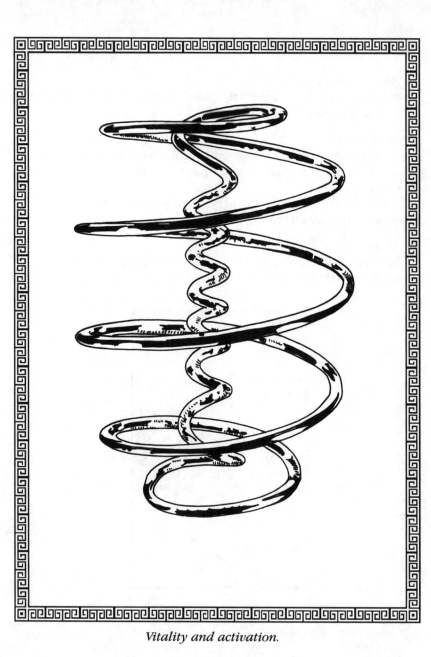

Vitality and activation.

DNA Double Helix

The DNA double helix is a more recent feng shui resource and is primarily used in the West. Because of the way it is constructed, with the inner and outer spiral moving in opposite directions, it is a symbol of the harmony that connects the universal opposites of yin and yang. The movement of the spiral creates a vertical beam of energy that unifies the energies of the earth (yang) with the energies of the heavens (yin). Suspended in a room, the DNA double helix emits a pulsating energy field that will harmonize and activate the energy in that space.

The spiraling double helix has captivated people in general for a long time, but has particularly fascinated children. The reason might well be that the basic building block of the human body—DNA (deoxyribonucleic acid)—has a double helix structure.

The outer helix is considered a yin helix when it turns to the left, and a yang helix when it turns to the right. The yin helix strengthens yin energy and the yang helix strengthens the yang energy in a room, in a ba gua area, or in a person.

Depending on its color (see Colors pages), the DNA double helix can also support a particular feng shui element and can be employed to activate a specific ba gua area.

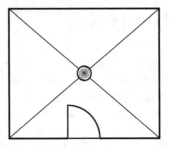

Applications:
• To stabilize and energize the center of a room, home, or other building (see drawing above)
• To activate and invigorate unused areas or rooms, like storage rooms, walk-in closets, bathrooms, etc.
• To improve yin/yang energies inside a room
• To connect two living spaces that are separated from one another by using a DNA double helix in each (one room with a yin helix, the other with a yang helix; see drawing below)
• To strengthen a person's determination.

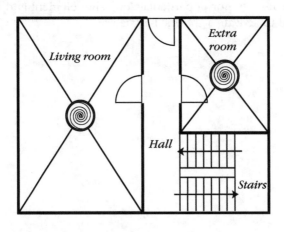

Ba Gua Areas:
- In all areas: a DNA double helix strengthens the specific area where used

Important:
- A DNA double helix should not be placed directly above a chair or bed.
- Make sure that the movement of the spirals is balanced and that it moves quietly.

Affirmation:
I am connected to heaven and earth and empowered by their pulsating energy.

Dolphins

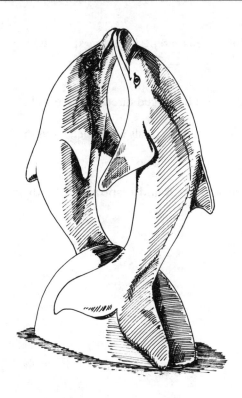

*Wisdom, peace, harmony,
responsibility, caring.*

The dolphin is a very intelligent marine mammal that seems to have a rare attachment to humans. Dolphins have caught the interest of people for centuries. Stories abound about dolphins who have saved human beings. One legend has it that the god Apollo took on the disguise of a dolphin in order to bring a shipload of Cretans to Delphi, where a temple was later built in his honor. Dolphins were also the signature animal for the ocean god Poseidon, and they are thought to have arranged his marriage to Aphrodite.

Aphrodite (Venus), born from the sea, is often depicted with dolphins. The Etruscans portrayed dolphins on gravestones and at burial sites, believing they were carrying the soul of the dead to the Island of the Blessed.

Other god legends state that the dolphin, the ocean-going mammal that is neither fish nor human, seems to be the mediator between heaven and earth. The animal also serves as a warning to people to treat the earth, nature, and everything alive with reverence, to use its treasures wisely and for the benefit of all. A few African cultures consider dolphins the equal of men and have given them the same rights that are accorded to people.

Dolphins enjoy life and are happy, playful, and very social. They are totally committed to their families. They learn early on to adapt to their community, to help each other. For example, a sick dolphin is constantly surrounded by other members of the family, who lovingly care for it.

All these traits have made the dolphin a very popular motif. Sculptures of dolphins alone, or in pairs as a symbol of mother and child, are made from a variety of materials (stone, semiprecious stones, or metal). They are used as garden sculptures, as talismans, and in jewelry. They grace indoor and outdoor fountains and are found on posters and pictures.

Regardless of where a dolphin is used, it is always a symbol of wisdom, peace, harmony, responsibility, caring, and universal love.

Applications:
• As a sculpture on a desk, to prevent ideas from being stolen
• As a poster in a child's room or in the office to promote a peaceful atmosphere.

Ba Gua Areas:
• Supportive Friends
• Children (dolphins at play)
• Marriage/Partnership (a pair of dolphins)
• Parents (a single dolphin, or a pair as a mother and child symbol)

Affirmation:
Every day brings joy. I am well, in harmony with life, and free.

Dragon

Energy, strength, prosperity.

The dragon is a well-known ancient symbol found in many Eastern cultures and almost always is depicted as a reptilian creature with a serpent's body, horns, wings, and fire-spewing breath. Excavations of artifacts in Pakistan and China date its appearance around the 4th century BC.

In China and East Asia, the dragon is considered a symbol of good luck. According to mythology, the dragon rests below the earth during the winter and appears again on the second day of the second month of the Chinese calendar. Its appearance brings about the thunder (the trigram of the east) and the first rainfall of the season, fertilizing the soil. In many parts of China the Dragon Festival is celebrated on this day.

A dragon with a ball or a pearl is also a symbol of nourishing rainfall. Since the dragon is a symbol of good luck, it is widely used as decoration on gates, roofs, royal flags, clothing, and many objects that are used daily.

The dragon and phoenix are symbols of masculine (yang) and feminine (yin) nature, respectively, and are used as the symbol of a married couple.

As one of the four heavenly animals, in feng shui the dragon stands for the east, the place of sunrise, spring, creation, and new beginnings—the reason it is also called the green dragon.

In feng shui, the dragon is the symbol of energy, strength, and prosperity. This makes it particularly important that the left side—the dragon side—of a house or property appear larger and more powerful than the right side. (In feng shui layouts north is considered to be down, so east is therefore left). To know which is left or right, stand with your back toward the turtle and look straight ahead (see pages on Four Heavenly Animals).

Inside the house, the dragon side needs to be more powerful. This can be accomplished with furniture, plants, or pictures.

In feng shui, a landscape is also explored to find the so-called dragon line, which may be in the form of a mountain crest, in order to determine where the most favorable location for a house might be. The optimal flow of *chi* can then be used.

Applications:
• When furnishing a room, larger objects, such as a large plant, cabinet, or dynamic picture, should be placed on the dragon side
• In the garden, the dragon side is emphasized by prominent objects, such as large trees, high hedges, a gazebo, or a rock garden
• In the form of a sculpture, a dragon talisman can be helpful in attracting good luck and perseverance.

Ba Gua Areas:
• Parents (thunder)
• Wealth (wind)

Affirmation:
With energy and gusto I surrender to the new (e.g., new day, new task) and trust my wisdom.

A pair of ducks: unity and fidelity.

Ducks

Since ducks in China are thought of more as a negative symbol, we will use the Mandarin duck, which enjoys a great deal of respect. In Europe you can find them in city ponds. They came originally from East Asia.

Mandarin ducks live in pairs for life, never changing partners. This makes them a wonderful symbol of a good marriage, and they are a favorite gift for couples. Decorated with a lotus flour and lotus fruit, a mandarin pair implies the impending birth of a son. A pair of mandarin ducks is considered a symbol of marital union and fidelity.

As an individual animal or a family, ducks are also the symbol of a caring mother and the connection to nature, the feng shui elements Earth and Water.

Applications:
• As a pair or group in sculptures or paintings.

Ba Gua Areas:
• Marriage/Partnership
• Parents

Egg

Mythology tells several different versions of how the world was created. One is that our planet was born from an egg. Greek mythology tells that many heroes came from eggs—e.g., the twins Castor and Polydeuces. The egg was the result of the union of Leda and Zeus; Zeus took on the form of a swan in order to be near Leda. A story from South Korea tells that a person found an egg with a infant inside who became the leader of all tribes.

In the south of China, legend has it that the egg brought forth the planet and all that is alive; after the great flood, however, the only survivors were two siblings. Finally the woman gave birth to an egg from which many children were hatched.

The egg in China, as in Europe, is the symbol of fertility. During a wedding ceremony, an egg is given to the bride and groom in many different forms. Sick people are also given an egg as a gift that expresses the wish for a speedy recovery. A child on its first birthday is often given a soft-boiled egg. On New Year's day, red-colored eggs are messengers of joy for the coming year.

In China and India, the egg stands for the unity of heaven and earth. In Egypt, the ankh also recalls the idea of the cosmic egg, which became a Christian tradition in the form of the cross.

In the West, pagan spring rituals used the egg as a symbol of reawakened animal and plant life. Christianity sees the egg as the symbol of resurrection—Christ rose from his grave on Easter Sunday (like a chick breaking through the shell of the egg). In the Christian world, people have colored eggs as decorations and had egg-rolling contests on Easter Sunday.

Applications:
• Decorated, as a wedding or New Year's gift
• As a symbol of fertility, to support the wish to have children
• As a hand-painted porcelain paperweight for growth and development.

Ba Gua Area:
• Children

Affirmation:
I connect to the energies of the universe in order to create something new.

Energy, strength, and wisdom.

Elephant

The elephant is the royal riding animal in Asia. In the past, in China, elephants were found in the way to the north, and in the southern provinces they have survived to this day. The elephant is considered a highly moral animal, as it was believed that it would mate only in the water, because it does not want to be observed. People also believe it knows the meaning of gratitude, because legends tell of a man who healed an elephant's wounds, following which the elephant gave its ivory to the man when he was sick.

A pair of elephants is often portrayed on either side of the tree of life, and paradise is seldom depicted without an elephant. In general, the elephant is an important animal symbol. He walks quietly with heavy feet, embodies earthly reality—Mother Earth, who patiently carries our burden and life's power—paired with great and undefeatable vitality, strength, and wisdom. If provoked, however, the elephant won't hesitate to show us who is the stronger.

Applications:
• As a sculpture or painted on cloth to express the characteristics of the elephant.

Ba Gua Areas:
• Knowledge
• Parents

Affirmation:
Energy, strength, and wisdom reside within me, and I am ready to let these qualities be expressed with lightness and joy.

Luck and a long life.

Endless Knot

The endless knot or braid is a very important symbol in China. The never-ending shape always turns back to itself. It is the Buddhist symbol of an unceasing, long life. The knot is also called a "knot of good luck." In China, the symbol is used in different and intricate forms (see lower drawing on opposite page).

Applications:
- As an individual border above the bed, for health and a long life
- As a border decoration along the ceiling.

Ba Gua Area:
- Could be in the Career area, as a wavy border

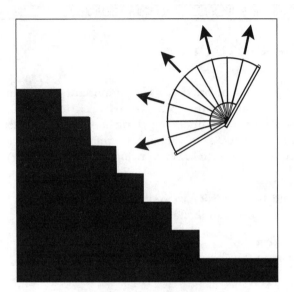

Energy is guided upward.

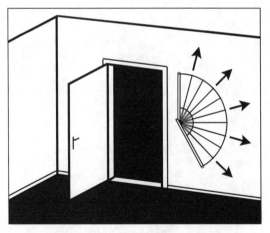

Energy circulating throughout the room.

Fans

Fans were known in China as long ago as 1000 BC and for a time were a sign of the rank of a civil servant. Chinese mythology states that one of the immortals (Chung-li Ch'üan) carried a fan that he used to bring the dead back to life. Some deities are depicted with a fan to drive out evil spirits.

In feng shui, fans are primarily for fanning, guiding energy in a desired direction. Even if hung on a wall, the fan's symbolic meaning will still serve its purpose.

The symbolic effect of a fan can be enhanced by the use of color, a motif (peacock, dragon, crane), or a calligraphic sign (luck, long life).

Applications:
• On a staircase, to guide energy upward
• In long hallways, to guide energy
• In large rooms, to improve the circulation of energy.

Important:
• The open side determines the direction of the flow of energy.
• Never point the fan straight up or straight down, but always at an angle.

Affirmation:
Energy is flowing, and I determine the direction.

Luck and joy.

Fat-Bellied Buddha

The fat-bellied Buddha became popular throughout East Asia during the Sung Dynasty (960–1280). Originally he was the embodiment of the Indian Buddha, Maiteya, who was to bring relief from earthly sorrows in the coming centuries.

He is portrayed as a happy, smiling, bald-headed, bare-chested man. He is the symbol of naive and unencumbered merriment. He promises to help us overcome the misfortune and misery of the real world.

The Chinese name for the fat-bellied Buddha is Mi-lo-fo. In Japan he is called Ho-tei and is supposed to be the god of peace and prosperity.

Application:
• As a harbinger of good luck and as an expression of joy.

Ba Gua Area:
• Wealth

Affirmation:
I am surrounded and filled with joy.

Prosperity and success.

Fish

In China, the fish is the symbol of wealth and prosperity, because the Chinese word *fish* is pronounced just like the word *abundance*. This has made the fish in Central China the favorite animal to be sacrificed to the god of wealth. It is also the reason why people in China eat fish on New Year's day, thinking that the coming year will be one of abundance.

Giving a card or a picture of a fish together with a lotus flower means: "May you live in abundance year after year."

Because of what the fish symbolizes, many people in China have an aquarium inside the house or a small pond outside, hoping to increase their chances for wealth and good fortune. No self-respecting restaurant in China will be without an aquarium. But it need not be an aquarium or pond. Aa picture, vase, shade, or porcelain figure of fish serves the same purpose.

In feng shui, fish—because of the shiny, sometimes colorful scales—are assigned to the element Fire and yang energy.

Applications:
• In an aquarium
• Depicted on a vase placed in the vicinity of the entrance to attract and accumulate good fortune
• As a porcelain figure, to attract wealth and prosperity
• In a picture or as a homemade clay sculpture, to attract wealth and prosperity.

Ba Gua Areas:
• Wealth
• Career

Affirmation:
Life will provide what I need and I am to enjoy it. Life gives to me in abundance, and I enjoy it.

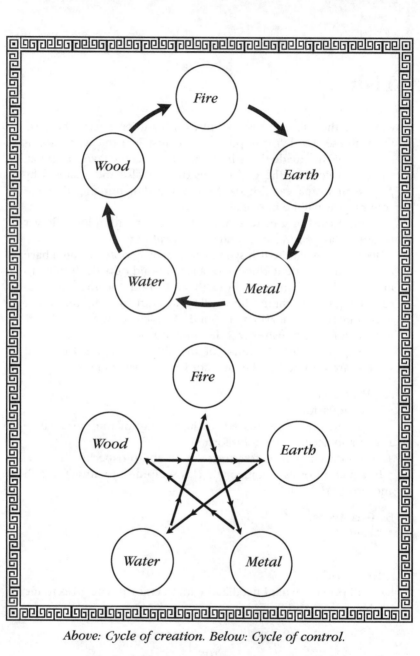

Above: Cycle of creation. Below: Cycle of control.

Five Elements of Feng Shui

The five feng shui elements—literally translated, "the phases of transformation"—incorporate everything that exists in nature: shapes, colors, matter, seasons of the year, times of day, directions of the compass, and all natural events, and structures created by man.

Together, the five elements represent a unit—the *tai chi*. Each element has its own particular characteristics:

Wood: developing, rooted, pliable, rising
Fire: soaring, in motion, hot
Earth: fertile, rooted, productive
Metal: hard, cutting, rigid, contracting
Water: flowing, cool, descending, supple

The specific power of each element can best be described in the following way: The nature of water is to moisten and flow downward; the nature of wood is to bend and be made straight again; the nature of fire is to blaze and ascend; the nature of metal is to be obedient and to be shaped; the nature of earth is to make things stable and steady.

It is important to remember that an individual element does not exist in isolation but is interconnected—either to be supportive, as in the cycle of creation, or to control, as in the cycle of control. They work in the following way:

Cycle of Creation:
Water nourishes wood, wood allows fire to burn, ashes created by fire nourish the earth, earth brings forth metals, liquid metal flows like water.

Cycle of Control:
Water extinguishes fire, fire melts metal, metal splits wood, wood wears out earth, earth dirties water.

Each element has different qualities or characteristics:

Wood:
- Tall, cylindrical, rising shapes
- Green
- Wood
- Spring/morning
- East
- Masts, towers, columns, flagpoles
- Creation, growth, creativity

Fire:
- Triangle and pointed shapes, sharp edges
- Red, violet, magenta, purple
- Leather, manmade material
- Summer/noon
- South
- Steep roofs, pyramids, columnar structures
- Expansion, intellect, inspiration

Earth:
- Flat and even shapes
- Brown, beige, yellow, orange, ocher
- Brick/tile, clay
- Late summer/late afternoon
- Center/middle
- Flat roofs, bungalows, terra cotta containers/vases, etc.
- Stability, safety, security

Metal:
- Round and ball-shaped forms
- White, gray, silver
- Metal
- Fall/evening
- West
- Rounded arcades, arches, dome-shaped roofs
- Concentration, thinking, precision, clarity

Water:
- Irregular and wavy shapes
- Blue, black
- Glass
- Winter/night
- North
- Irregularly shaped structures or buildings with a lot of glass
- Communication, flexibility, conviviality

Recognizing these characteristics makes it possible to evaluate the energies of an environment or an individual living space and to recognize the influence they have on a person. It also makes it possible to change things to improve the sense of wholeness.

In feng shui, the five elements are extremely important because—depending on individual preferences and needs—we can effect change where we live through the use of colors, shapes, and designs. The atmosphere in a bedroom could be enhanced by the use of quiet colors and shapes. In a living room or dining room, we can use more lively colors and shapes to increase a sense of joy and vitality.

Feng shui allows us to put together the right combination of elements or cycles of elements for a specific situation or circumstance. We can, for instance, reestablish harmony with the control cycle when one element dominates. *Good combinations* are:
- wood/fire/earth • metal/water/wood • fire/earth/metal.

111

Flag of the Chinese emperor (until 1912), a yang symbol.

Flag

First and foremost, a flag was a strategic aid used as a signal to communicate orders to distant places. Later the flag became a symbol of honor and dignity. In Europe, flags were used to signal that the march to victory had begun. The flag became a prominent symbol in coats of arms.

Chu Hung-wu, the founder of the Ming Dynasty (1368–1644), went with his army into battle with a red flag. After he had declared himself the emperor he changed the color of the flags to yellow. Yellow was considered the color of the emperor.

In feng shui, flags have a different meaning. As a moving object, the flag symbolizes yang energy and attracts *chi*—-the reason flags are so popular with large firms or businesses. They are also used for festivities, business openings, or to call attention to something or someone in the world outside.

Applications:
• As an advertisement tool to attract potential customers
• As garlands and focal points for special sales
• As announcements of specific events
• As an identification tool for the world outside.

Important:
To avoid uneasiness, the flagpole should not be located opposite the entrance door.

Energy contibutor.

Flowers

"Say it with flowers" is an idea that we all have in mind when we buy flowers, consciously or unconsciously. A rose is an expression of love, a forget-me-not is a remembrance, and a bouquet of flowers marks a special occasion. All follow a long-standing tradition. Flowers speak their own language, depending on the color and shape and the season they represent. They can express a mood and brighten up any room.

Flowers connect us with the energy of nature. In Japan, arranging flowers has been elevated to an art, in which people attempt to simulate the perfect harmony between heaven and earth. Blossoms, twigs—even dried flowers and fruit baskets—represent the rhythm of nature: living and dying, birth and death, action and quiet.

In China, the flowers of the four seasons are: iris or magnolia for spring, peony or lotus for summer, chrysanthemum for fall, and plum blossom and bamboo for winter.

Flowers and plants are excellent for transferring *chi* energy, particularly when they are in full bloom and healthy. Dried arrangements should be replaced periodically, particularly when they become dusty.

Applications:
- To make wonderful table decorations, perfect for any occasion
- To convey a secret message
- To activate and energize the flow of *chi*
- To symbolize life and impermanence
- To express joy.

Ba Gua Areas:
Flowers are suitable for any and all areas as well as to express a specific mood or thought in a particular area:
- Knowledge: lilies (innocence and wisdom)
- Marriage/Partnership: roses (love)
- Parents (bamboo shoots for a long life)
- Supportive Friends: forget-me-not (faithfulness)
- Fame: sunflowers (expressing radiance)

Affirmation:
I am connected to the energy of flowers and live in harmony with nature.

Flutes

A flute produces wonderful, harmonious sounds. In the past, flutes were used to announce peace and bring good news. This has made flutes the symbol of peace and safety.

In feng shui, flutes are used to redirect the flow of energy in a specific direction or to bring the cosmic energy of *chi* into a room. When using flutes, it is important to pay attention to where the mouthpiece is pointing, because the opening determines the direction in which the air is being blown.

Flutes are always used in pairs. Some come with painted or carved motifs, which add to their symbolic meaning. If they have a dragon and phoenix motif, the dragon always needs to be on the right side when seen from the front. The flutes are mounted at a 120° angle to each other. The length of the flutes and the distance between them should be chosen according to the favorable measurements chart of feng shui (see the Measurements pages).

Applications:
• Inside, above the entrance door (see the drawing on the left) as a protection against negative influences or to allow the cosmic energy of *chi* to enter the

house—with the mouth-piece pointing up.

• Mounted on a wide ceiling beam, to counteract the downward-pressing energy (see drawing at right), with the mouthpiece pointing down.

• On the staircase, to guide the upward-moving energy back into the room—mouthpiece pointing down.

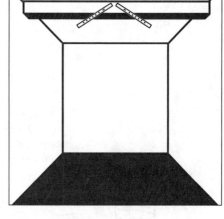

• Below a sharply angled sloped ceiling or wall, to redirect upward-moving energy back into the room, with the mouthpiece pointing up.

Important:

• Do not mount a flute on or near a window.
• The end of the flute should never point at a person (or his bed, desk, etc.).

Affirmation:

I am surrounded by peace and harmony—I am fulfilled.
Everything in my life is good.

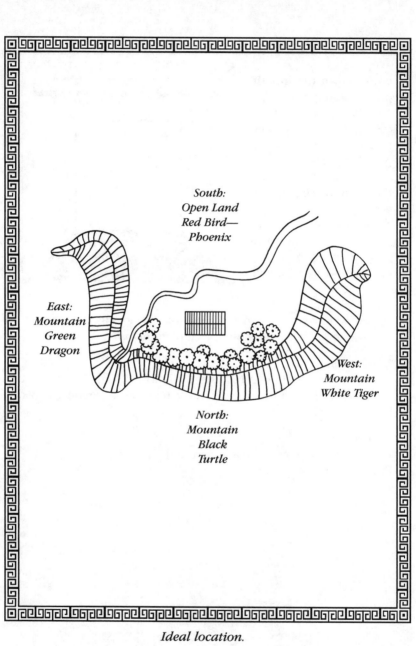

Ideal location.

Four Heavenly Animals

"Where the dragon and the tiger embrace, there is *chi.*"

The above simple sentence is an example of how the four heavenly animals influence the environment, according to feng shui. Each house or place derives its character based on the way the surrounding area is designed. In feng shui, the symbolism of the four heavenly animals can be described as follows:

Turtle
The turtle protects the back of the house or property and assures serenity, stability, and safety.

Dragon
The dragon rules the left side (left if you are inside, facing the front) of the house or property, and should be prominently displayed. As the guardian of the house, the dragon assures good luck and prosperity.

Tiger
The tiger rules the right side of the house or property, and should look more gentle and be smaller than the dragon. An overly large tiger might cause bad luck and strife.

Phoenix
The phoenix is placed at the front of the house or property and must be able to fly unencumbered, so the area must be flat and open. The phoenix assures joy and honor in life.

If all four characteristic energies of the four heavenly animals are in place, you can say in feng shui terms that you have the ideal location. This is true for the whole house as well as for the individual rooms.

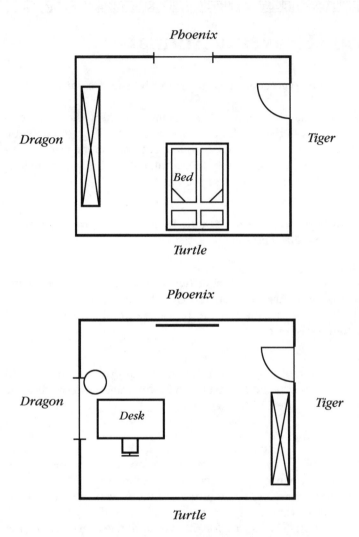

Above: Ideal location for a bed. Below: Ideal location for a desk. The strength of the dragon is increased by a strong plant (circle).

The point from which a building or room is viewed is always from inside looking out with the turtle protecting the back, and you would look straight ahead at the phoenix. That puts the dragon on your left and the tiger on the right. On closer inspection, you might see the whole in the shape of a horseshoe—a symbol of good luck and prosperity (see opposite page).

Inside a room, we look for the best place for a bed or desk. Like a comfortable armchair, a solid wall should be the backdrop, with the sides of the room providing comfort and support and an open and unencumbered space in front.

Applications:
• When buying or renting a house or apartment, see if it is possible to have all the attributes of the heavenly animals present
• When furnishing a bedroom, make sure that there is good protection in the back (turtle) and a free and open view in front (door/window)
• For the desk: do not sit with your back to the door, but always against a solid wall.

Order and structure.

Four Heavenly Animals Mobile

This mobile depicts the four heavenly animals that represent the four directions of the compass. The dragon stands in the east, the phoenix in the south, the tiger in the west, and the turtle in the north.

Through their attributes, these four animals impart the principal energies that represent the fundamental powers of nature. They connect us to the order, balanced structure, simplicity, and clarity of nature.

This makes the animals mobile particularly suited to areas of orderly and structured energies or places where these attributes are missing—for instance, in a child's room, kitchen, study, office, or place where you meditate.

Applications:
The effectiveness of this mobile can be greatly enhanced by combining it with other symbols, depending on the effect desired:
- To achieve stability, with a crystal globe
- To block loss of energy, with a wind chime
- To activate an area, with a double helix.

Ba Gua Areas:
- All areas

Health improver.

Fragrances

Fragrances have been used for medicinal purposes, in aromatherapy, and in perfumes since time immemorial. They are also used to enhance the atmosphere in rooms. The quality of the air influences the way we feel and how much energy we have, usually without our being aware of it.

When tension is so high that "the air can be cut with a knife," we feel ill at ease or are in a bad mood. Fresh, clean air and a pleasant fragrance will mobilize our spirits and allow us to breathe freely and more deeply.

Fragrances can invigorate, refresh, calm or cleanse, depending on which essential oil is used. There is something for each occasion and every need.

Feng shui offers several possibilities to improve and revitalize the atmosphere in a room and the quality of the air (with a diffuser, as in the drawing on the left). It is important to pay attention to the quality of the essential oils or fragrances. Make sure that the essential oils are of the highest quality and each fragrance pleasant to the nose.

Since essential oils are dispersed in the air by evaporation, the application and symbolism of a fragrance belongs to the feng shui element Fire.

Applications:
• With a diffuser, to disperse essential oils and fragrances
• Spraying essential oils directly into the air for a quick cleansing or revitalization of a room.

Ba Gua Areas:
• Fame: refreshing and happy fragrances
• Marriage/Partnership: soft and warm fragrances
• Knowledge: fragrances that improve concentration

Life-transforming quality; fertility.

Frog

The frog is a symbol of emerging and life-transforming qualities and fertility. This animal is particularly interesting because it changes from an egg to a tadpole to a four-legged form.

Folklore has assigned countless abilities to the frog, and no witch's kitchen is complete without a frog. It was believed that a frog would impart the power to magical potions. Emerging from the dark and unknown depths of a well or bog into the light of sun, the frog can change evil into goodness and beauty, attributes that have made the frog a symbol of resurrection and healing.

Applications:
- As part of an outdoor water fountain
- As a sculpture inside the house or added to flower arrangements
- As a sculpture on the windowsill or the winter garden
- As part of an indoor pond.

Ba Gua Areas:
- Career
- Children

Affirmation:
I accept with joy the possibilities of transformation and growth.

Protection.

Glass Globes

Glass globes have resurfaced as favored decorations in front yards and backyards and are very effective feng shui remedies. They defend against harmful influences *(sha chi)* in the environment and can be used to attract positive energies.

Colorful glass globes act like convex mirrors, reflecting the surrounding space and nurturing the *chi* around it.

Applications:
• To invigorate a specific area in the garden as a color accent
• To minimize negative influences (like sharp corners) in the garden or a planter
• In pairs on each side of the front door or gate (as guardians), to attract positive or deflect negative energy
• To decorate or invigorate the center of a garden.

Ba Gua Areas:
• Everywhere, according to need or liking; choose the color according to the nurturing feng shui elements (see Five Elements of Feng Shui pages) needed in an area.

Important:
The glass globe must be kept clean at all times to assure continued effectiveness.

Well-being.

Golden Fruit

Artificial and real fruit painted gold are a symbol of nourishment, well-being, and life. Who would not love to sit down and enjoy such fruit? Fruit is a favorite gift to bring when visiting a sick friend. Savory fruits are nature's way of sweetening the road to recovery.

Golden fruit, made from wood and then painted gold or layered with gold foil, is particularly decorative. The gold color makes the fruit more powerful and valuable. Placed in a black bowl, they become a symbol of "the noble attracting the precious." This combination is a favorite feng shui remedy.

Application:
• Arranged in a black bowl, gold attracts or expresses prosperity and abundance.

Ba Gua Area:
• Wealth (in the kitchen or dining room).

Greek Key Pattern
(Meander)

Rebirth and eternity.

A Greek key pattern or meander, symbolizing the flow of a river, often is found in stylized form as a border decoration on rugs, ceramics, and walls. A meander is similar to the Chinese sign for "returning," thus it is also a symbol of rebirth and eternity.

Individual representations vary greatly. Often a meander is made up of squares, spirals, or swastikas folded into one another. The constant repetition makes it a symbol of eternity.

In feng shui, the Greek key motif can be used to create a particular effect in a room, underlining the theme that has been chosen.

Applications:
• In a bathroom, as a tile border
• As a pattern for a wallpaper border or for curtains
• As a creative, decorative finish (for a wall, border, etc.).

Ba Gua Areas:
• Career
• Wealth
• Parents

Abundance and good fortune.

Horn of Plenty
(Cornucopia)

The horn of plenty was a kind of mythical drinking implement from which a never-ending supply of vegetables, fruits, flowers, and other gifts of nature appeared. It is associated with plants, earth and fertility as well as the goddess Fortuna. This makes it a symbol of the gifts of the gods, who give to people without asking them anything in return.

In prehistoric times, the horn was often used as a sacrificial vessel. It is also the symbol of hope.

Applications:
- As a container, filled with gold-painted fruit
- As a decoration, with flowers and fruit.

Ba Gua Area:
- Wealth

Affirmation:
Everything in the universe is available to me in abundance.

The three house gods: Luk, Fuk, and Sau.

House Gods

The three most important house gods in China are Fuk, Luk, and Sau—the divine triple star. They can be found in almost every Chinese home all over the world.

Fuk

Fuk is the god of prosperity and good luck. In his hands, he holds a scroll that contains the formula that summons the kindness of fate. He is the largest of the three and always stands in the middle, which underscores his importance.

Luk

Luk is the god of honor and abundance. He holds a scepter of power and authority in his hands.

Sau

Sau is the god of good health and long life. A high, protruding forehead is his special characteristic. He holds a peach in one hand and a walking stick (with dragon motif) in the other.

Fuk, Luk, and Sau are always grouped together and are given a place of honor—sometimes even their own room—in the house. Make sure that their place of honor is always taller than any table in the vicinity. Their presence guarantees constant prosperity, health, and abundant food.

The house gods come in many different sizes and shapes, some as colorful porcelain or ceramic figures, others in the form of valuable gold statues.

Applications:
• In the vicinity of the entrance, to favorably influence incoming energy (favorable fate)
• In the living or dining room for favorable fate
• In a place of honor within the house.

Ba Gua Areas:
• Everywhere

Affirmation:
May this house be filled with the blessings of prosperity, health, and honor.

Incense

People have burned incense for cleansing purposes and ritual ceremonies for a long time. In addition to incense, some of the most popular items used during ritual ceremonies are bark, resins, roots, leaves, and flowers. The most precious substances were reserved to honor the gods. Thick billowing smoke would rise from incense-burning vessels, carrying the plea for protection and well-being to the beyond where the gods live. Fragrant smoke has always been a fascinating symbol of life, death and transcendence.

In China, incense burning is a long established tradition and has many applications. Incense is burned to provide pleasant fragrances for rooms and clothing, to communicate with the gods, and to drive out evil spirits. Burning incense during *I Ching* readings is an absolute must, because it creates the right atmosphere in which to receive the divine wisdom or the pure breath of the gods.

In Japan, the *koh-do* (way of incense burning) was usually celebrated under the guidance of Zen monks. Different royal families conducted full-blown incense burning feasts.

In more recent times, aromatherapy uses a variety of fascinating fragrances as a way to touch the soul. Feng shui burns incense to cleanse or remove negative energies from a room or home and has given this ritual new meaning. Daily incense burning is highly recommended in places where *sha* (negative) energies are particularly strong, as in sickrooms, waiting rooms, places used for meditation or therapy, etc.

Specialty shops carry a great variety of products used for incense burning, including the appropriate vessels, charcoal, and sand. If you don't like the odor of charcoal, a wire grid suspended over a vessel can be substituted. A tea light provides the necessary heat.

Applications:
• Before moving into a new home or house
• After an illness or conflict
• Anytime, depending on individual preferences, or as a regular ritual
• Daily, as support during meditation or relaxation.

Affirmation:
I am cleansing my space from everything that is out of balance and turning towards light. I am letting go of the past and living peacefully, with joy. I am relaxed, allowing life to flow through me with lightness.

Life and vitality.

Indoor Pond

Moving water symbolizes life and vitality. It attracts *chi* energy like a magnet and provides energy for life.

Bubbling water in an indoor pond is a constant source of moisture for the air; it filters out dust particles from the air and ionizes the air with vital negative ions, all of which add to physical and emotional well-being.

The water should move gently over the stones and should produce a soft bubbling sound.

When putting an indoor pond together, remember these rules:
1. Arrange stones and plants in places where the plants will thrive.
2. Make use of the cycle of 5 feng shui elements in your choice of shapes, colors, and objects.
3. Try for a good yin/yang balance.
The above suggests that the container for the pond needs to be big enough to create a sufficiently large water surface. Stones and plants ideally should be arranged to symbolize a tiger, dragon, phoenix, and turtle (see pages on Four Heavenly Animals).

It is important that the water always be clean and the plants, healthy and strong. The technical parts—such as the pump, lights, and filters—need to be in good working order as well. We recommend that you use only filtered water (with a charcoal filter) to reduce lime and other unsightly deposits on the stones, plants, and the container.

Applications:
• To provide and increase vital energy to rooms
• As a humidifier
• To activate "dead" corners and areas
• As a focal point at the entrance to an office or business.

Ba Gua Areas:
• Wealth
• Parents
• Career

Important:
• Always make sure that the water is clean and the plants healthy.
• Don't place objects next to the fountain that belong to the Fire element.
• Don't place the fountain in front of a window.

Affirmation:
I surrender to the flow of life and am willing to give and receive.

Mercy.

Kuan Yin

Her full Chinese name is Kuan Shi Yin Po Sa, which translates as: She who hears the screams of the world. Originally she was a *he:* the Buddhist sun god Avalokiteshvara (the patron of Tibetan Buddhism), a bodhisattva who with his thousand hands and thousand eyes lived in the sun, the home of truth.

Portrayed according to the ideal of beauty in India, he began to look more and more like a woman, with fully developed breasts. This is probably the reason why, in China, people saw him as a goddess (documented around the 9th century) and considered Kuan Yin to be the goddess of mercy, compassion, and of manifest knowledge. She knows when someone needs help and brings peace and empathy wherever she may be.

Applications:
• As a porcelain figurine she has a dragon at her feet that can be filled with water. After meditation, the water can be sprinkled throughout the room to disperse her energy
• As a sculpture carved from wood, to attract the energy of peace and mercy.

Ba Gua Areas:
• Helpful Friends
• Knowledge

Affirmations:
May there always be peace and empathy in my house.
I am at peace and possess compassion.

Labyrinth in Chartres.

Labyrinth

The labyrinth is one of the most important geomantic shapes. It should not be confused with an ordinary maze. A labyrinth is a one-way path that always ends at the center of the circle. Moving through a labyrinth collects the energy in this space and sets it free. It is the symbol of the human journey from birth to death and resurrection—with all its trials, tribulations, delays, and complications.

One very famous labyrinth is in the cathedral of Chartres, France (see drawing on the opposite page). It measures 39 feet (12 m) in diameter.

The labyrinth was almost forgotten, but in the early 1970s many cities rediscovered labyrinths when they built new plazas and marketplaces. Designers used labyrinths to mark the center of a plaza. More and more garden and landscape architects are also using this motif in order to increase vitality and energy.

Applications:
- In a garden, as a lawn design, with gravel or box trees
- In entrance halls, with colorful flagstones
- In larger buildings, as a focal point.

Ba Gua Area:

- In the Center

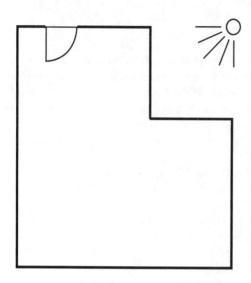

Light

Light is energy, and the greatest source of light is the sun, whose energy makes all life on earth possible. In feng shui, bright, warm light is the basic requirement for the presence of sufficient life energy *(chi)*.

The quality and proper choice of lighting is very important. Dark rooms inhibit the flow of *chi* and contribute to depression and discomfort.

Balancing a missing area with light.

The same room can come to life, filled with energy, if the right lamps are chosen.

With different sources of lighting—like wall and floor lamps, spots or indirect lights—it is possible to create very specific effects, according to the use of the room. It is important that lamps and lights are placed so that people in the room are not bothered by the glare.

A good feng shui application would be to illuminate entrance areas, doors, and the path leading up to the home. This increases the flow of *chi,* making it easier for energy to reach the home. Restaurants and hotels frequently use of this kind of illumination, trying to draw customers to their establishments.

Full-spectrum light is most effective. It contains the colors of the rainbow and positively influences the health of the people living in the home. Regular incandescent light bulbs, while not as effective, are also all right.

Try to avoid fluorescent or neon lights and low-voltage halogen lamps, particularly in living rooms, bedrooms, children's rooms, and offices. They have a negative influence on people.

Applications:
- In rooms with dark corners, to increase the flow of energy
- To counteract the oppressive effect of low, dark ceilings
- In windowless places, to increase energy flow
- To illuminate an entrance to a business, to attract the attention of potential customers
- To illuminate walkways, to guide the flow of *chi*
- In L-shaped structures, to balance the "missing area."

Ba Gua Areas:
- Fame
- Any ba gua area where *chi* needs to be improved or increased

Important:
Replace any defective lamps immediately.

Affirmation:
Light is flooding into my life and brings joy.

Purity.

Lily

The lily in Christianity is the symbol of virgin love and is used in religious processions as a sign of purity. Gabriel, the angel of the Annunciation, is usually depicted carrying a lily. For many saints, the lily is the expression of complete perfection.

As the royal flower, the fleur-de-lis, the lily is the most important motif in heraldry. Legend has it that an angel gave Emperor Chlodwig I of France (481–511) a lily. Since 1179, the lily has been part of the coat of arms of the Royal House of France.

The pleasant fragrance of the fully open blossom of the lily is very good for feng shui. In China, people believe that this plant lets you forget all your worries. As a gift for a young woman, the lily is an expression of the wish that she may receive the gift of a son, which makes the lily a very popular wedding or birthday gift. In addition, an iris is hung on the front door on the fifth day of the fifth month as a defense against evil spirits.

Applications:
• As a decorative plant
• As a stylized emblem on walls, furniture or fabric.

Ba Gua Area:
• Fame

Courage and strength.

Lion

The lion is the king of the animals, and because of his impressive mane, courage, and strength, he has been considered by many cultures a symbol of the sun.

His masculine magnetism made him the quintessential opposite of goddesses. Many a hero had to overpower a lion in order to demonstrate his strength and the ability to defeat his animalistic nature. This is also quite often depicted in Christian art.

As the king of the animal world, the lion stands for battle and power and was used as a heraldic animal as early as the Middle

148

Ages. In Europe—for example, in Bavaria, Sweden, and earlier in Great Britain—the lion, as a symbol of power, is represented in many coats of arms. In Christian art, the most well-known image is a lion with wings—the symbol of the Evangelist Mark. The lion is also represented in the coat of arms of Venice.

In Western astrology, the lion stands for fire, the sun, and gold. People born under the sign of the lion (Leo) love life, luxury, and wealth, and have a tendency to be vain and theatrical; they love family, have leadership qualities, and are domineering and autocratic.

When kings and people of authority wanted to display their wealth, power, and prestige to the outside world, they would place sculptures of lions at the entrances to their houses or in the palace garden. The lions informed everybody entering that this was the residence of an important person who demanded respect.

In China, the lion is a symbol of protection for the entrance to a building. The lion pair always stands outside the front door to protect against bad luck entering the house. Entrance gates that are guarded by lions are also called lion gates.

Applications:
• As a guard next to the entrance door (to the home or garden)
• On a picture or banner at the entrance door.

Ba Gua Areas:
• Career
• Supportive Friends
• Family
• Fame

Affirmation:
Courage and strength will protect this house.

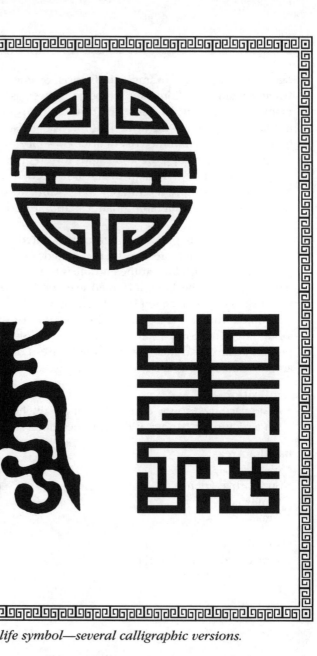

Long life symbol—several calligraphic versions.

Long Life Symbols

To reach old age in good health and be able to enjoy the fruits of one's life is for many Chinese people the most important aspect of good luck. Countless variations of the long life symbol exist, and all are representations of this worthwhile goal.

What follows are the most important symbols. More detailed explanations can be found on the pages for each topic in this book.

Gods:

Shou-hsing:	god of longevity
Sau:	god of long life
P'eng-tsu:	the Chinese Methusaleh

Animals:
Stag
Crane
Turtle

Plants:
Bamboo
Pine tree
Peach

Applications:
• As sculpture (of a god or animal) inside the house
• As plants in the garden.

Ba Gua Area:
• Parents (health)

Affirmation:
I trust that life will bring only good things.

Innocence and enlightenment.

Lotus

The lotus flower is one of the most important symbolic plants in China. It is the symbol of innocence. It stands for Buddha's enlightenment and occupies a special place in the philosophy of Buddhism.

The lotus grows in muddy, marshy water, but it seems that in spite of this its flowers are brilliantly beautiful, which is why it is the symbol of immaculate beauty and virgin innocence in an unclean environment.

The lotus in China has two names, *lien* and *ho*. In Chinese, *lien* is pronounced like the words for "connecting," "loving," and "uninterrupted," but also "humility." *Ho* stands for "unity." Together with other symbols, many plays on words are created. For instance, a young boy with a fish and a lotus next to him means: "May you have abundance, year after year." Two lotus plants are a symbol of marriage: sharing harmony and one heart.

In feng shui, the lotus is a favorite plant for a pond, because it is thought to bring good luck when in bloom. If it bears fruit, it means that the house will receive an abundance of good luck.

Applications:
• As a plant in the pond, like the water lily
• As a Chinese painting
• As a stylized ornament on walls or decorations.

Ba Gua Area:
• Marriage/Partnership

Magic Squares

Magic squares are squares that have been divided into 9 equal sections in which numbers have been placed in such a way that the sum of the vertical, horizontal, and diagonal numerals is always the same. Magic squares are well-known in Far Eastern and Western mysticism, and originated in India. In China the magic square is called the *lo shu*.

The following legend is known in feng shui and Chinese numerology: King Fu Hsi (2500 BC), a very wise man, sat down on the banks of the river Lo to meditate, when a turtle appeared from the water. On her back was a pattern of colored dots (or water

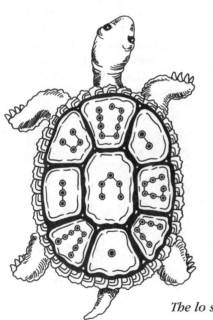

SE	S		SW
	4	9	2
E	3	5	7	W
	8	1	6
NE	N		NW

*Note: The feng shui convention is to put north at the bottom of the compass.

The lo shu -- security and power.

drops) that were arranged like the numbers in the magic square. He became convinced that this design explained the movement of energy in the universe. This square is known to this day as the *lo shu*, or the plan of the Lo River.

The *lo shu* serves as the basic structure for many calculations in feng shui. It is for instance the starting point for the ba gua or the eight trigrams, as well as the basis for the 9-star *ki*, also known as the flying stars—astrological calculations and analysis for people and buildings. The *I Ching (Book of Changes)* was developed by King We (around 1000 BC) from the *lo shu*.

In the West the magic square probably got its name because people used it in charms or amulets. Magic squares were assigned to represent certain planets, as the value of the sum represented the attributes of the particular planet, which is why they are also called the "seals of the planets."

Saturn

Saturn's is the smallest planetary magic square. It is made up of 3 × 3 squares. The basic numbers from 1 through 9 always add up to 15. This square is supposed to have been engraved into the signet ring of Solomon and as an amulet was to have conferred power and security on him.

4	9	2
3	5	7
8	1	6

The Saturn square.

Connecting the opposite corners and sides of the square through its center recreates the hagal rune (see the pages on Runes).

155

Jupiter

Jupiter's square consists of 4 × 4 spaces, and the sum of the digits in each row or column is always 34. In Western astrology, Jupiter stands for good fortune, insightfulness, and faith. The square is said to provide wealth, peace, and harmony.

4	14	15	1
9	7	6	12
5	11	10	8
16	2	3	13

The Jupiter square.

Mars

Mars's square is divided into 5 × 5 spaces, and the sum of the digits of a row or column always is 65. In Western astrology, it stands for assertiveness, spontaneity, and dynamism. The square is supposed to grant success, vigor, and health.

Applications:
- As a charm for protection above or next to the entrance door
- As an emblem or talisman.

11	24	7	20	3
4	12	25	8	16
17	5	13	21	9
10	18	1	14	22
23	6	19	2	15

The Mars square.

*The mandala: A depiction of the order of the universe
(cosmogram).*

Mandala

The word *mandala* comes from Sanskrit and means "holy or
magic circle." The symmetrical connection among several circles
and squares creates many different shapes and patterns that are
used in meditation and to aid concentration.

Originally the mandala was used to depict the order of the universe—it was a cosmogram. The circle represented the heavens, and the squares, the four corners of the compass. Its cosmic power was transferred to architectural designs and the construction of temples.

The best-known mandalas in the West are those created in Tibet, where the center is often a lotus flower with a god figure inside. The symmetrical shape of a mandala conveys a sense of harmony and balance, which creates an intimate sense of peace and tranquility.

A mandala can be painted on a wall or on silk fabric, or carved out of wood, and may be created according to one's own intuition or imagination. Mandalas are also painted with colored sand or powder on the floor. Sand mandalas are done for very specific rituals and at the end of the ceremony are destroyed and given back to nature.

Applications:
• As a picture or wood carving, hung on the wall to invite cosmic energy
• As a floor design at the entrance or hallway, to attract cosmic energy into the home
• As a floor design in the center of the house, for peace and tranquility.

Ba Gua Areas:
• Knowledge
• Career
• Center

Affirmation:
Life is abundant; it is generous and promises knowledge and wisdom.

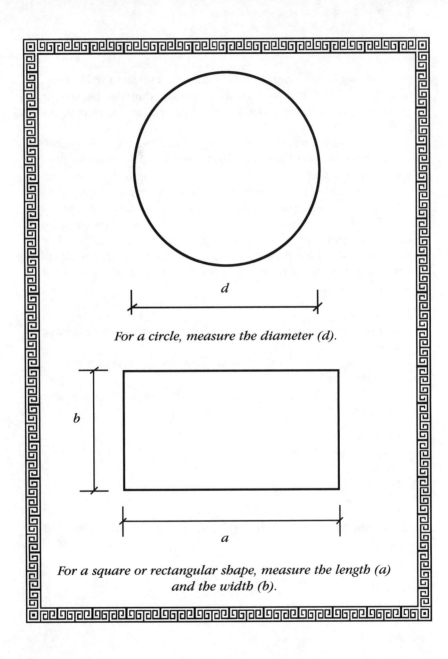

For a circle, measure the diameter (d).

For a square or rectangular shape, measure the length (a) and the width (b).

Measurements

Each object, like every color and every form, vibrates in its own, specific way. Depending on the size and proportions of an object, these vibrations affect us either favorably or unfavorably. We can often tell if an object is well balanced or not because we all have an innate feeling for it.

The Chinese measuring system was established in the Sung Dynasty (960–1279). A furniture builder designed and made the furniture for the royal family according to these rules, and they are still valid to this day. Many feng shui practitioners in China and Hong Kong use these measurements when they design office furniture, furniture in general, and other things.

The *ten lan,* a ruler or measuring tape, is the tool that workmen use in determining favorable or unfavorable proportions. The measuring unit of these rulers is unique. The length is 1 *chih* (1 feng shui foot), or 42.96 cm (16.9 inches), which corresponds to the diagonal of a square where one side measures 1 Chinese foot (approximately 30.3 cm) or 11.92 inches. The feng shui foot, according to the *I Ching* or the 8 trigrams, is divided in 8 sections, and each section (1 *tsun*) measures approximately 5.4 cm (2.12 inches). After the eighth section, the whole cycle is repeated, so the 8 sections can be applied to every measurement.

In China, people have great respect for the dimensions of an object. It is no accident that a briefcase in China corresponds exactly to the feng shui measurements. They ensure success, luck, and growth, and people believe that the measurements will favorably affect what is inside.

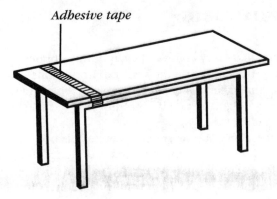

Adhesive tape

If the measurements of a table are unfavorable, adhesive tape—even underneath the tabletop—can be used to divide the table into harmonious sections.

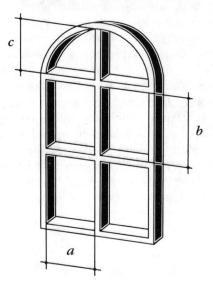

c

b

a

To determine the proportions of a sectioned window, always measure the inside (the opening) of the section.

Favorable and Unfavorable Measurements

Sections	Size (in.)	Size (cm)	Area	Meaning
1	0–2.11	0.–5.37	*Ts'ai*	Lucky measurement
2	2.12–4.22	5.38–10.74	*Ping*	Illness
3	4.23–6.34	10.75–16.11	*Li*	Separation
4	6.35–8.45	16.12–21.48	*I*	Luck through helpful people
5	8.46–10.57	21.49–26.85	*Kuan*	Strength
6	10.575–12.685	26.86–32.22	*Chien*	Bad luck
7	12.69–14.79	32.23–37.59	*Hai*	Harm
8	14.80–16.91	37.60–42.96	*Pen*	Capital

Mirrors

An old Chinese saying states: "A mirror makes illusions visible." We know of so-called magical mirrors in which mystical symbols appear on the back if the mirror is held and looked at from a certain angle. Buddhist monks use magical mirrors to show believers in what form they will return to this world after their present life is over. Some cultures believe that a mirror is a symbol of marital happiness and good luck. Should a mirror break, it means separation and divorce.

While mirrors in the distant past were made from polished metal—often silver—today they are made from glass. As with all remedies, in feng shui it important to remember that a mirror also has a back side. If the mirror is in the wrong place, it is possible to attract bad *chi*. If the mirror is too large, positive *chi* can be thrown back.

Mirrors are primarily used to influence the flow of *chi*. Since a mirror reflects *chi*, a dead corner can be reenergized by the way a mirror is placed. But no matter how or where a mirror is used and in what direction it is pointing, it always influences, guides, or increases the flow of *chi*. For that reason, to maintain a tranquil atmosphere it is recommended that you avoid using mirrors in the bedroom.

There are many different ways to use mirrors. We list a few possibilities below, based on the effect desired.

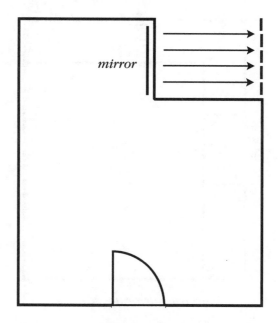

mirror

Mirror to balance L-shaped room.

1. Balancing Missing Areas

Today's modern space designs often have missing areas in the layout of a room or building from a feng shui point of view, which interferes with the harmony and balance of the occupants. Mirrors give us a means to open up a room, making it appear larger than it really is. In feng shui, mirrors are used to balance missing areas.

In the case of an L-shaped room, a mirror is placed on the wall facing the missing area. The illusion of depth symbolically dissolves the wall, and the missing area becomes available.

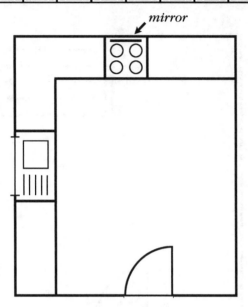

mirror

Rearview mirror above stove.

2. Rearview Mirror (for Protection)

When a person is sitting at a desk or standing at a stove with his back turned to the door of the room, he unconsciously feels unprotected and perceives the place as being uncomfortable. The consequence often is a lack of concentration or a meal that does not turn out well.

If rearranging furniture so the person can face the door and have his back protected is not an option, a small "rearview" mirror at the desk or above the stove can be the remedy. Just like the rearview mirror in a car, it will improve the overall view and provide a sense of control. At the desk, a paperweight with a vertical mirrorlike surface or a picture with a reflecting surface could provide a less obvious but equally effective solution.

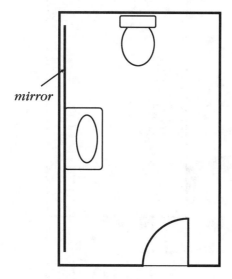

mirror

Large mirror in small bathroom.

3. Enlarging Rooms

Small bathrooms often present a problem, which is worse if the room is without a window. The flow of energy is stagnant. But here, too, we have an answer: a large mirror will instantly provide a sense of the space. The flow of *chi* is stimulated and the flow of energy is restored.

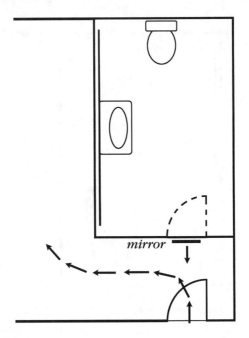

Mirror outside a bathroom door near an entrance.

4. Blocking Doors

Sometimes bathroom or closet doors are right next to or opposite the entrance door. This situation allows a considerable amount of energy to escape, producing an energy vacuum in the home. As a remedy, place a small mirror at eye level on the outside of the doors leading to these rooms. They will guide or reflect the flow of *chi* and thereby prevent the loss of energy. Ordinary mirrors will do, but a door sign with a reflective surface or golden sun symbols also is effective.

5. Balancing Offset Doors

Doors located diagonally to each other are a no-no in feng shui, because this causes loss of energy, which can disturb the harmony and balance in a home. Two small mirrors can remedy the situation; they are placed next to each door (see drawing), which balances the tension and guides the flow of *chi* in healthy ways.

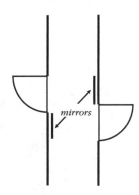

mirrors

6. The Doubling Effect

Mirrors reflect everything, in a sense doubling the objects placed in front or opposite them. This effect can be use to increase wealth and prosperity.

In the kitchen, the oven is the symbol of the finances of the household. A mirror placed above it or next to it is said to double the home's prosperity.

Businesses often have a mirror close to the cash register in the hope that each bill received or already in the cash register will be doubled.

Important:
• Mirrors need to be cleaned regularly so that they reflect only clean energy.
• No mirrors in bedrooms—they disturb peaceful sleep.
• In dressing rooms, use only one-piece mirrors—the person looking into the mirror should never appear as if cut in half or into sections. This is also true for bathroom mirrors.
• The size of a mirror should be proportional to the size of the room.

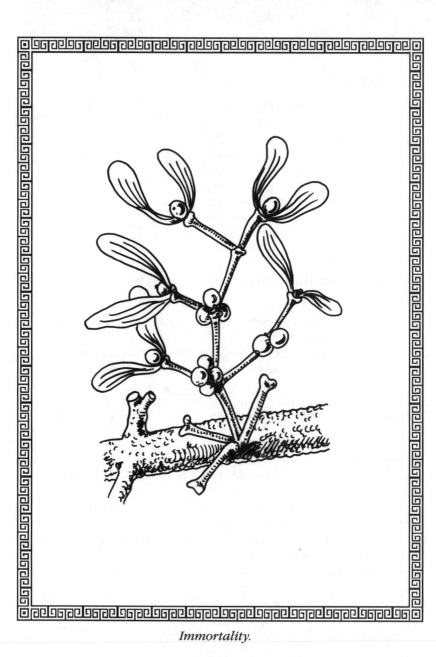

Immortality.

Mistletoe

Mistletoe is a semiparasitic plant, and its peculiar growth habit made it a holy plant in the West.

The Celtic people noticed that this plant feeds only on very particular hosts—for instance, the oak tree. This plant is neither tree nor bush and its leaves are always green. The fruit ripens during the winter. It needs light to germinate, but grows best in darkness and in the vicinity of water, never becoming waterlogged.

Mistletoe follows its own destiny and is very different from the ordinary world that surrounds it. It seems to be connected to a more mystical plane of existence. Celtic people followed a very specific ritual when harvesting this plant. Taking the phases of the moon into consideration, white-clothed Druids cut mistletoe with a golden sickle during sacred ceremonies and wrapped the mistletoe in white cloth. Afterwards a steer was sacrificed, and the mistletoe was presented to the gods.

The plant was believed to heal every known sickness and prevent infertility in man and beast. Mistletoe has been proven to lower blood pressure. It is also a diuretic. Anthrosophical medicine (Rudolf Steiner) uses substances from mistletoe for cancer-prevention.

Because of its evergreen leaves, the plant also became a symbol of immortality. The thick juice of its berries was supposed to have rejuvenating powers. In some countries, mistletoe is suspended above the entrance door during the Christmas season, when the berries are ripe. It is supposed to bring good fortune to the people in the home. Legend has it that kissing under mistletoe will bring good fortune for lovers, but anybody can be kissed without repercussions when caught standing under the mistletoe.

Application:
• Above the entrance door during Christmas time, for good luck for the coming year.

Balance and harmony.

Mobile

A mobile, moved by the air currents in a room, stimulates the circulation of *chi* and brings harmony into rooms with weak energy flows. Its three-dimensional arrangement distributes energy evenly in a room. This makes a mobile particularly effective in places with little movement—for instance, in a room with so-called dead areas or corners.

In addition to activating energies, mobiles are used to reduce or slow the flow of negative energy *(sha chi)* when suspended in front of large windows or in long hallways. Depending on its motif, a mobile provides specific effects, which can be made to suit each individual situation.

A special kind of mobile (see drawing) is called "harmony wing"—several colorful pieces of wood of different sizes are connected on a string. Like other mobiles, these also energize the flow of *chi* in a room.

Different kinds of mobiles and their meanings:
- Fish: prosperity and abundance
- Dolphins: love and harmony
- Birds: freedom and lightness
- Butterflies: change and transformation.

Applications:
- In rarely used rooms (storerooms, guest bathrooms, etc.)
- In dead corners, to activate energy
- In front of large windows, to reduce the flow of energy
- In long hallways, to slow the flow of energy.

Ba Gua Areas:
- Marriage: Dolphin mobile
- Fame: Butterfly mobile
- Wealth: Fish mobile

Affirmation:
I am connecting to the lightness of being.

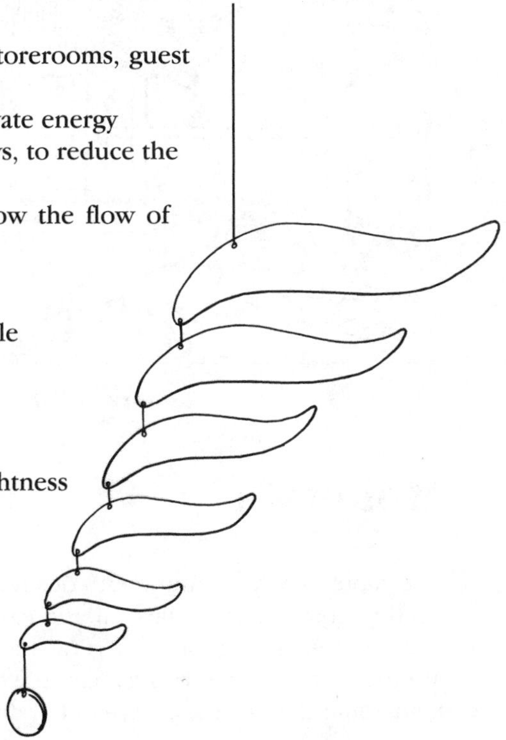

Stability and wisdom.

Mountain

The mountain has long been considered a symbol of the connecting point between heaven and earth, the place were we are nearest to God. A mountain is also a symbol of human ascent. Mountains are seen as rising above the condition of mortal human beings and therefore are a symbol of divine power. Many cultures and cities claim their own sacred mountains. They are perceived as an eerie and frightening passage to a superhuman, intimidating world. Pilgrims to sacred mountains have likened their journey to this higher spiritual plane to a step-by-step process of letting go of the concerns of everyday life.

The ancient Chinese belief in the five sacred mountains, based on what they see as the five points of the compass (east, south, west, north, and the center), is still valued today. Since ancient times, the five mountains have been honored as places of sacrifice: in the east the T'ai-shan; in the south, the Southern Heng-shan; in the center, the Sung-shan; in the west, the Hua-shan; in the north, the Northern Heng-shan. All five mountains are covered with trees—a rarity in China—and several Taoist temples have been erected at the summit. Almost every mountain had its own mountain god. In the past, people believed that the souls of the dead lived in these mountains.

Today, mountains are considered a symbol of the connection between heaven and earth, of wisdom, stability, and the slow and arduous ascent towards spiritual awareness.

The trigram Keeping Still is expressed in feng shui through mountains.

Applications:
• As a poster, painting, or photograph
• As a large boulder in the garden
• In the form of a crystal lamp to create a relaxed atmosphere.

Ba Gua Area:
• Knowledge

Affirmation:
I trust my inner wisdom and walk through life one step at a time.

Support.

Mythical Beings

Many of us can still remember the giants, elves, gnomes, fairies, and other mythical creatures from the early days of our childhood, which came to life when Mom or Dad read us those exciting stories, fairytales, and fables. They are our invisible helpers who watch over us.

Some people are able to communicate with fairies—each person in her own way. Since the willingness to entertain such possibilities is steadily increasing, we can work with these beings, whether we can see, feel, or hear them or only have a sense that they are around.

Mythical beings can help us gather the energies necessary for successfully growing flowers, bushes, trees, and plants in the pond or garden, on the terrace or balcony, and inside the house.

We should approach them seriously and with respect and—when necessary—ask for their help.

Applications:
To gain support, you can place painted or unpainted ceramic, clay, or metal figurines (like elves) at specific locations in the garden or next to a vase or flowering plant in the house.

Ba Gua Areas:
• Supportive Friends
• Children: for increasing creativity

Affirmation:
I ask for the energies of nature and its creatures to support me.

Numbers in the East

In China, the symbolism of numbers applies to a whole complex of situations and emblems. This enables one to connect similar systems with different numbers, to complement the philosophy that nature is always changing. When interpreting the meaning of numbers, it is important to know that the meaning will differ from region to region depending on the dialect.

In feng shui, all even numbers (2, 4, 6 ...) are counted as ying and all uneven numbers (1, 3, 5 ...) as yang.

 One

In the East, one stands for loneliness and bad luck, for authority, and for things that will definitely happen. But one is also a spiritual number that represents the highest, the most superior, the *tai chi* from which the two principles of yin and yang came into being. One is assigned to heaven.

 **Two**

Two is considered a positive number and stands for unity (yin and yang) of opposites and reciprocal trust. Its pronunciation sounds much like the word "simple"—implying that what we hope for can be accomplished without effort. Two is assigned to Earth.

Three

Three is also considered a positive and meaningful number. Pronounced, it sounds much like "lively," thus the attributes of growth and the promise of many descendents are assigned to three. A favorite magical feng shui symbol consists of placing three coins under a healthy plant in order to nourish wealth. Three is assigned to human beings.

Four

In China, four is the most negative number and is avoided wherever possible, because the pronunciation of "four" sounds like the word "death." As a protective measure, a circle surrounds it and contains its negative energy.

Number Combinations:
- 24: It is easy to die.
- 74: Dying is inevitable.

Five

Five is a positive as well as a neutral number. It is the number of the middle. In China, it is an important mystical number. Five, for instance, is the number of the phases of transformation (see the pages about the Five Elements), and of the directions (north, east, south, west, center). In the Mandarin dialect the pronunciation of "five" is much like that of the word "nothing," which is why some feng shui traditions avoid this number.

 Six

Six is the number for good luck and a symbol for property, wealth, and abundance. It is pronounced much like the word for "rolling" or "motion," which means it provides good conditions for moving towards wealth and abundance.

 Seven

Seven is considered a holy number. Its pronunciation in Chinese sounds much like the word "certain," which gives special meaning to combined numbers.

Number Combinations:
- 78 = Becoming is a certainty.
- 74 = Dying is a certainty.

In mystical numerology, seven is assigned to the woman. She lives according to a 7-year rhythm:
- 7 months: Baby teeth
- 1 × 7 years: Loss of baby teeth
- 2 × 7 years: Beginning of menstruation
- 7 × 7 years   End of menstruation

八   Eight

In feng shui, eight is the ultimate number of good luck because its Chinese pronunciation sounds just like the words for "blossoming, growing" or "wealth." A horizontal eight is the symbol for infinity, harmony, and prosperity. Eight embodies the order in nature—in the eight trigrams or the eight directions of the compass. Eight is a favorite for house and telephone numbers, or a number on a car's license plate.

Number Combinations:
• 28: Getting rich is easy and fast.
• 78: Becoming wealthy is certain.

Eight is assigned to the man; he lives in an 8-year rhythm:
• 8 months   Baby teeth
• 1 × 8 years   Loss of baby teeth
• 2 × 8 years   Beginning of fertility
• 8 × 8 years   End of fertility

九   Nine

Nine is the number meaning "long life," because when pronounced in Chinese, it sounds like the word "longevity." Nine is also considered a lucky number and is another favorite for number combinations. In the magic square, nine is in the south, the most important and beneficial direction in feng shui.

Number Combinations:
• 289: It is easy to have wealth for a long time.
• 99999: Infinity (multiple longevity)

181

Numbers in the West

Our world consists of numbers and has from the very beginning. Numbers are a mirror of reality. Each individual number has its own reality, quality, and spiritual symbol. Every culture has developed its own interpretation of numbers.

In the West, primary importance was given to the order of the universe. We came to believe that everything in nature is created according to a specific rhythm: in music we have 7 basic tones, in architecture the golden mean (3:5:8), and in the world of plants there are characteristic numbers of flower petals. The symbolism of numbers also influenced the way facades and decorative additions were included in the design of important buildings. This is particularly evident in the numbers of arcades and statues, and in the detailed measurements used in designing rosette windows.

In feng shui, all even numbers (2, 4, 6 ...) are considered yin, and all odd numbers (1, 3, 5 ...) are yang.

1 One

The one stands for undivided singularity, the source and root of all numbers. It stands for creation, progress, individuality, oneness, and self-development. This number is assigned to the sun.

2 Two

Two stands for duality and dichotomy, as well as reciprocal attraction. Recognition and knowledge are created by balancing and connecting opposites. Two is assigned to the moon.

3 Three

Three is the number of wholeness and completeness and the symbol of God. It symbolizes body, mind, and spirit or consciousness, unconsciousness, and divine consciousness. It also stands for the family: mother, father, child. It represents love of life, optimism, and openness. Three is definitely considered a lucky number and is assigned to the planet Jupiter, the messenger of good luck.

4 Four

Four is the traditional number of the earthly universe, the elements, the seasons, the direction of the compass, and the square. It is associated with solidarity, stability, drive, and endurance. Four is assigned to the planet Uranus.

Sun wheel,
symbol of the
four seasons.

5 Five

According to Pythagoras, five is the most complete number of the microcosm, the human being a pentagram. Human beings react via the five senses: hearing, sight, taste, smell, and touch. Five is considered active, impulsive, adventurous, curious, and inventive. It is assigned to the planet Mercury.

6 Six

Six is the number of days it took God to create the world, which gives superhuman power to this number. Its attributes are balance, health, and peace, empathy, love, and duty to the community. Modern interpretation holds that it symbolizes partnership. It is assigned to the planet Venus.

7 Seven

As in Asia, in the West seven is considered a holy number. It symbolizes the divine Trinity (3) in the earthly universe (4). Seven represents the mystical change of birth and rebirth. We know of the seven sacred vows and the seven deadly sins. Seven belongs to the planet Neptune.

8 Eight

Eight represents the flow of life's energy in an endless spiral motion. A horizontal eight is the symbol of infinity. The number eight expresses strength, power, and authority. Eight belongs to the planet Saturn.

9 Nine

Any number from 1 to 8 when multiplied by 9 equals a number whose numerals total 9 when added. For example, $4 \times 9 = 36$ and $3 + 6 = 9$. Nine is therefore called "the number of perfection." The square of 9 is 81, "the number of eternity." It expresses generosity, tolerance, empathy, and freedom. Nine is assigned to the planet Mars.

Love and beauty.

Orchid

More than 2000 years ago, the poet Chu Yuen compared the virtuous character and graceful manner of the orchid to that of a graceful lady. In general, this flower is the symbol of love and beauty. In China, the fragrance of the orchid is compared to the breath of a beautiful woman. Depicted alone, it symbolizes purity, virtue, and innocence.

Orchids in a vase mean "harmony." The *I Ching* states, "Two people living in harmony diminish harshness, because words spoken in harmony carry the fragrance of orchids."

Applications:
- As a potted plant or in a vase as a gift after an argument
- As a Chinese painting (see opposite page).

Ba Gua Area:
- Marriage/Partnership

Affirmation:
We walk through life in love and harmony.

Knowledge.

Owl

The symbolism of the owl is mixed. People in the distant past perceived darkness as negative and dangerous, full of uncertainty, and therefore connected to evil and bad things. This bird of the night—unsocial, with a mournful call and silent flight—was considered a bad omen. The owl was seen as unpredictable and was thought to be the messenger of death.

On the other hand, its calming manner, large eyes, thoughtful and seemingly inward-looking gaze, and its extraordinary night vision made the owl the symbol of Athena, the goddess of wisdom and science. This might well be why some bookstores and publishers use the owl in their firm's logo as a symbol of erudition and wisdom.

Applications:
• As a wooden, stone, or porcelain sculpture
• As a woodcut.

Ba Gua Areas:
• Knowledge
• Parents

Affirmation:
I trust that I will have the necessary knowledge when I need it and that I am able to use it wisely.

Creativity and intuition.

Paperweight

Paperweights that are glass globes containing spirals, air bubbles, flowers, or abstract objects increase creativity and intuition in work. As feng shui remedies, they work well on a desk at home or at the office. In a child's room, in the ba gua area allocated to Children, the paperweight supports growth and joyfulness.

Applications:
- On a desk: to increase creativity and intuition
- In a child's room: to support development

Ba Gua Area:
Children: on desk or in child's room

Important:
Before you activate the Children area, the area must be cleaned up and orderly.

Affirmation:
I welcome imagination, new thoughts, and ideas.

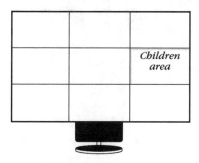

Paperweight location on desk.

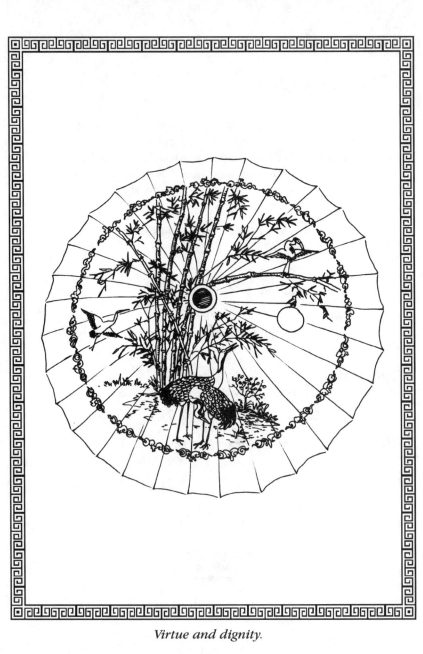

Virtue and dignity.

Parasol

In China, the collapsible parasol has been used for more than 2000 years. By parasol, we don't mean the kind that is popular in the West. The Chinese parasol is one of the eight symbols of Buddhism. It stands for dignity and is a symbol of the virtue of a civil servant. In many pictures an umbrella is held over a person of honor.

The parasol is also used during wedding ceremonies as a shield for the groom, and a parasol is suspended over the bed of a child for protection, support, and help.

Parasols frequently are artfully decorated and brightly painted, and are very popular as decorative objects.

Applications:
• Depending on the motif, suspended in corners to activate the area. When placing the parasol, make sure that the decorated side is always visible, regardless of whether that is the inside or outside.

Ba Gua Areas:
• All areas

Beauty and youth.

Peach

The peach was brought from the Orient in the 1st century AD. In China, it is the strongest symbol of immortality and longevity.

The peach blossom is the symbol of young innocent girls, but also of capricious, easily seduced women. The expression "peach blossom foolishness" refers to the confusion of puberty.

The wood of the peach tree was believed to ban demons. This gave rise to the tradition of placing peach tree branches in front of the house on New Year's day to keep evil spirits away. The wood was also used to carve divine gate guardians that were placed in front of the gate for protection.

One of the most important house gods—Sau—holds a peach in his hand as a symbol of immortality.

Applications:
• Arranged in a fruit bowl in the kitchen or on the dinner table
• In a Chinese painting.

Ba Gua Area:
• Parents (health)

Affirmation:
May health and well-being reside in this house.

Freedom and love of life.

Phoenix

The symbolism of the Chinese phoenix *(feng-huang)* should not be confused with that of the one we know in the West. The Chinese phoenix has nothing to do with rising from a cleansing fire. In China, the phoenix is thought to be the god of the winds. Part of its name, *feng* ("wind"), was adapted by the people who developed feng shui.

The body of the phoenix is a symbol of 5 human qualities: the head stands for virtue; the wings for responsibility and duty; the back, for correct behavior; the chest, for humanness; and the belly, for reliability.

Some texts speak of a cinnabar-red phoenix who was born in a cinnabar-red cave at the South Pole, and was called the Phoenix of the Cinnabar Mountain. This might be why feng shui speaks about "the red phoenix" or "the red bird."

Depictions of a dragon and a phoenix stand for the masculine (yang) and the feminine (yin) in nature, and together are the symbol of a married couple.

As one of the four heavenly animals, the phoenix stands for south (the direction of strongest yin energy), the day, and summer, as well as strength and action.

In addition, in feng shui, the red phoenix is the symbol of freedom, the sun, recognition, and trust.

Since the phoenix is able to observe everything freely from the air, the front of the house (the basic direction of a house) should be open and uncluttered. This provides powerful yang energy for the house. A gently flowing creek in front of the house would also be ideal.

Applications:
• When furnishing a room, it is important that the entrance to the room is open and uncluttered.
• When designing a garden, try to keep the area at the front of the house flat and planted with low-growing plants. Among other things, the front of the house is an ideal place for a pond.

Eternal friendship, durability, long life.

Pine Tree

The evergreen pine tree appears to be fresh and bright, even when very old. It is the most popular tree in Chinese art. Because it survives even the coldest winter and never sheds its needles, it is a perfect symbol of eternal friendship, durability, and long life. The tree has a similarly prominent place in Chinese poetry. Confucius wrote about the pine tree: "Its stillness is what lengthens its life."

Together with the plum and the bamboo, the pine tree belongs to the "three friends of winter." A pine tree depicted together with a crane symbolizes the last years of a long life. This makes the pine tree a favorite to plant at a grave site. Decorating the house with a pine branch and green plants during the cold and harsh days of winter is an ancient Chinese tradition, which is not unlike the symbolism of the evergreen tree at Christmas in the West.

Feng shui favors pine trees' being planted at the entrance to the house or the garden. However, they should not grow too tall when mature, and should blend harmoniously with the total design.

Applications:
- As a pair, potted next to the entrance
- As larger individual trees at the back of the house. Here the pine tree can take over the function of the black turtle (protection).

Intensifying energy.

Pinwheel and Windsock

Pinwheels and windsocks are primarily used outside, in the garden, on a balcony, or on a terrace. Their perpetual motion, even when there is hardly any wind, attracts attention and thereby energy. They activate energy and vitality in the space around them.

Windsocks are now constructed from weather-resistant materials and can be used throughout the year.

Applications:
• To balance a missing area on a balcony or terrace
• To activate a specific ba gua area in the garden
• To attract attention and as a focal point at the entrance door.

Important:
Windsocks need to be functional at all times and should be repaired or replaced when they become damaged.

Plants

Plants come in many varieties and shapes and include trees and shrubs, annual and perennial plants, and flowers. Plants are used outside in the garden and as decoration inside the home. The possibilities are endless. What follows are the tips and suggestions for their use that we feel are most important.

Plants as Living Organisms and Energy Sources

Plants have their own energy fields which, depending on the type of plant and its growing habits, is different for each. Many people communicate with their plants and feel stimulated, safe, or fascinated in their presence. Scientific research has confirmed that there is indeed a kind of telepathic interaction between humans and plants—proof of how much plants influence our physiological and psychological well-being.

Healthy, strong plants provide a great deal of energy in the space in which they live. The vitality and strength of plants is ideal for increasing *chi* energy indoors.

Plants as Air Filters and Humidifiers

Plants are also excellent in dealing with polluted air (dust, paint, cleaning solutions, certain appliances, wall-to-wall carpets, etc.) by taking in the carbon-dioxide-filled air and returning oxygen to the air. They improve the quality of the air in a room, increasing an overall sense of well-being.

Chrysanthemums, gerberas, and ferns are excellent for dealing with formaldehyde. One plant even is able to filter acetone, benzoin, and trichlorethylene from the air. The moisture released by plants increases humidity indoors, which makes for a more comfortable indoor climate.

Plants as Protectors

By strategically placing one or more plants, we can literally create a protective shield. This could be outdoors to protect the back of the house, or to neutralize a dead corner outdoors or indoors. It is important, however, to chose the right plant. Plants with sharply pointed leaves, like the yucca palm, should be avoided because the shape of the leaves sends out poisonous arrows, according to feng shui beliefs. Ivy, bamboo, and philodendron are ideal.

Feng Shui Elements Assigned to Plants

Wood: Columnar plants, those with upward-growing habits, climbing plants

Fire: Plants with cylindrical growth and/or pointed leaves and thorns

Earth: Plants that remain wide and low, ground covers, plants whose leaves or branches point down

Metal: Plants that have ball-shaped, round, or half-round growing habits—either naturally or by training

Water: Irregularly growing plants with wavy leaves.

Placement and Care

Each plant or tree, indoors or out, needs a special place and special care to remain healthy and strong. Only then can their beauty and energy be of benefit to people. When buying a plant, pay attention to care instructions and get expert advice if you are unsure.

Symbolism of Plants

We usually have a very distinct reaction to or attitudes about plants, particularly about popular or native plants. Buying and placing a plant in a certain area often expresses very personal needs.

In general, plants with sharply pointed leaves, such as yucca palms, aloe plants, or agaves, are considered detrimental because the shape of the leaves expresses or conveys a don't-touch-me energy. For that reason, it is recommended that such plants should not be placed in bedrooms, and placed in living rooms only where they can be far away from seating areas.

Bonsai

Bonsai plants, originally grown in Japan, can be considered from

two points of view. On one hand, the process that keeps the plant small—namely drastic pruning—greatly reduces its *chi* and thereby its strength and vitality. On the other hand, in spite of such drastic treatment, this plant has enough vitality to persevere and grow.

Ivy

Ivy, because of its ability to attach itself so securely to structures and objects, stands for friendship and is an expression of constancy and patience.

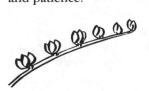

Forsythia

This plant, which blooms in the early spring, is a symbol of vitality, optimism, and joy.

Fuchsia

The magenta flowers of the fuchsia plant look like little lanterns and provide strong yang energy, which is why the plant is a symbol of good luck.

Jade

The jade plant—because of its fleshy, round leaves that look like coins—is one of the most famous symbols of wealth and prosperity. It takes almost ten years for a jade plant to produce flowers, and then it happens only under specific conditions. But once in bloom, money will begin to flow into the house. This plant also represents the energy of patience and reliability.

Hibiscus

The profusion of blossoms of the hibiscus plant connects us to abundance, fame, and wealth.

Cactus

Cacti use their prickly spines to protect themselves against uninvited or dangerous visitors. What an example of how to keep one's boundaries! What a reminder of how important the word *no* is when we need to defend our boundaries. The magnificent flowers they produce also remind us of the beauty hidden in the unassuming and simple.

Magnolia

In China, a magnolia tree in the front yard is a symbol of contentment and good fortune. The same tree in the backyard points to hidden jewels or consistently increasing wealth.

Narcissus

In China, this plant is called "eternal water" and is brought into bloom for the New Year. It promises good fortune.

Cypress

The cypress is an evergreen plant that, in Europe, is frequently seen in cemeteries. Since they grow upright and live to be very old, cypresses are a symbol of long life and solemnity.

Plum blossom knot, symbol of the five petals of the plum blossom and the five gods of good luck.

Plum

"A few branches of a plum tree in bloom. Defying frost, they quietly unfold their flowers. In the distance, it is clear it can't be snow. A sweet fragrance comes from somewhere."
—*Wang An-shih, 11th century*

This poem describes the blossom of the plum tree, East Asia's favorite symbol of the early years in a young girl's life. Its delicate flowers begin to appear even before the tree unfolds its leaves.

In China, the plum tree stands for the five gods of good luck *(wu-fu)*. The three trees—the pine tree, the bamboo, and the plum tree—comprise the three friends of winter, because none of them dies, all three are dependable, and they begin to bloom even before spring starts.

The blossom of the plum tree has symbolic meaning in several areas. A flowering branch from a plum tree arranged in a bowl or vase is like a messenger of spring.

Applications:
• Plum blossom branches: As table decorations, a messenger of spring
• Plum blossom knot: As a wall ornament to invite good luck (see drawing opposite page).

Affirmation:
I am ready for the promise and energy of spring.

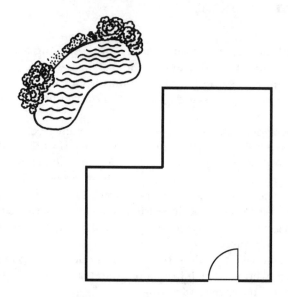

*A pond in the garden to balance a
missing area of the house.*

Pond

A pond in a garden represents the feng shui element Water and as
a feng shui symbol brings wealth and prosperity to the occupants
of the house. A pond stocked with fish is ideal for bringing good
fortune.

When designing a pond, be sure to pay particular attention to
the following:

• A pond needs care, which is time-consuming; if you don't have
the time it is better to discard the idea because muddy, brackish
water attracts bad luck and financial and health problems.

- The size and shape of the pond have to fit harmoniously into the environment. A pond should not be too small or too large. At a maximum it can be as large as the house.
- To keep the pond ecologically balanced, add water plants, grasses, and fish—all of which help to keep the water fresh and clean.
- A stone or boulder in the pond allows water to move gently about, creating a relaxing atmosphere.
- A fountain in the pond increases vitality and stimulates, particularly if the fountain is illuminated.

Applications:
- On your land, to strengthen the feng shui element Water in the environment
- As a symbol of wealth and prosperity
- To add yin (a calm pond) or yang (a pond with a fountain)
- As part of a garden design, to balance a missing area of the house (for instance, when the Wealth area is missing).

Ba Gua Areas:
- Wealth
- Career (with moving water)

Important:
- The water in the pond has to be kept fresh and clean.
- Do not place a pond on the right side of the house (right when seen from the inside).

Wealth.

Rainbow

A rainbow—one of the wonders of the sky, which seems to physically connect heaven and earth—is a symbol of revelation in many cultures. In Greek and Roman mythology, Iris is the goddess of the rainbow and the messenger of the gods (see drawing on the opposite page). The colored part of our eyes, the iris, is named after this goddess.

In Christianity, the seven colors of the rainbow stand for the seven sacraments and the seven gifts of the Holy Ghost. The rainbow is also the symbol of reconciliation.

Legend says that there is a pot of gold at the end of the rainbow. Ancient Celtic coins were often called little "rainbow bowls."

Applications:
• As a wall decoration in living or bedrooms to allow the vitality of rainbow colors to brighten your life.

Ba Gua Area:
A rainbow, which contains all the essential colors, can be used in every ba gua area.

Affirmation:
I am connecting to the energies of heaven and earth to the very center of my being.

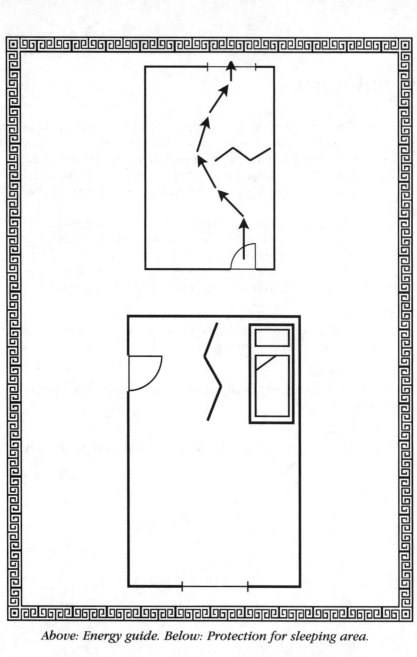

Above: Energy guide. Below: Protection for sleeping area.

Room Divider

Folding screens or room dividers are used in feng shui to guide the flow of *chi* or to protect or shield particular areas. A room divider needs to be adjusted to each specific situation. If a great deal of protection is needed, the material has to be strong (for instance, wood). The divider is always placed at right angles to the negative energy flow or to the *sha* arrow.

A room divider is also a wonderful way to separate a desk and workspace within a bedroom, or to create a quiet, secluded zone in a living room.

Applications:
• To break a straight energy flow from the entrance to the back door
• To shield a sleeping area from a door in a small room, such as a child's room
• To divide living areas from sleeping areas.

Affirmation:
I feel protected and safe.

Eternal love.

Roses

In antiquity, the rose was the symbol of rebirth and of love that could reach beyond death.

In Christianity, the rose has several different meanings. It is considered the symbol of the blood of the crucified, and therefore is the symbol of divine love. Five-petal roses have been carved in confessionals. The white rose, the queen of flowers, stands for Mary and virginity. In the Middle Ages, wreaths made from roses could be worn only by women who were still virgins.

In literature, the rose to this day is still the flower of love. Alchemists believed that white and red roses stood for sulfur and mercury and were symbols of duality. A rose with seven petals is considered a symbol of the seven metals.

Many fraternal organizations chose the rose as an expression of their spirituality—like the combination of a cross and the five-petal rose of the Rosicrucian Order. For the Masons, the rose is the symbol of secrecy, beauty, and virtue, and the expression of love, light, and life.

Applications:
• As a bouquet, to express affection and love
• As potpourri, to enjoy the fragrance of the flower
• As stylized symbols on borders in the bedroom.

Ba Gua Areas:
• Marriage
• Fame (red roses)

Affirmation:
I am willing to be open to love.

Runes

Runes are letterlike characters that were used for writing and other communications by the Northern European Germanic tribes. Many scholars believe that their origin dates back to Greece. Runes and rune-like inscriptions can be found on cave walls, weapons, and jewelry in southern Europe (Portugal, France, and Crete), as well as in the British Isles, India, and northern China. Some of these inscriptions are estimated to be from 5000 to 10,000 years old, or even older.

Knowledge of runes in Anglo-Saxon areas was confined to priests and sorcerers. Individually, runes were thought to possess magical power, and all runes are closely related to transcendental energies and cosmic powers.

Rune	Name	Meaning
ᚴ	*Fa*	Guidance
ᚫ	*Ur*	Comprehension
ᚦ	*Thorn*	Goal
ᚭ	*Os, Othil*	Proposal
ᚱ	*Rit*	Bygone
ᚤ	*Kun*	Existing
✳	*Hagal*	Eternal change
ᚼ	*Not*	Separation
ᛁ	*Is*	Course
ᚠ	*Ar*	Transition
ᛃ	*Sig*	Determination
↑	*Tyr*	Agitation
ᛒ	*Bar*	Fertilization
ᛚ	*Laf*	Destiny
ᛉ	*Man*	Desire
ᛦ	*Yr*	Completion
ᛉ	*Eh*	Association
ᚵ	*Gibor*	Achievement

With the arrival of Christianity, runes were considered part of pagan religions. They were first frowned upon, then repressed, and finally forbidden and burned, forever destroying irreplaceable records. Oral traditions have kept this secret wisdom alive through the centuries. With the rise of fascism in Germany, which used runes as political symbols, the status of runes got even worse, and runes are viewed with suspicion to this day.

A physicist in Austria believes that runes are symbolic representations of the flow of cosmic energy. He considers three possibilities:

• The vertical flow of energy represented by straight vertical lines, as in the *is* rune.

• The union of two energy flows as they cross one another, as in the *eh* and the *not* rune.

• The confluence of three energy flows, as in the *hagal* rune.

These three basic flows of energy are accompanied by contiguous flows and expressed by half-strokes, as in the *fa, kun,* and *laf* runes.

Applications:
• As a protective or energy symbol at the entrance door
• As a symbol in company logos or coats of arms.

Wall anchor— German man.

Tension in a hexagram created by the hagal rune.

Semiprecious Stones

Semiprecious stones are created by crystallization, erosion, and oxidation. Because of their structure, mineral content, and the resulting colors, they create very specific, radiating effects. Their harmonious system carries information that is transmitted to the environment. They communicate with us on a vital, vibrational level.

For an exchange of energy to take place, it is important that stones are not crowded and are in a place where they can be seen.

Different semiprecious stones in their natural state and shaped and polished by man can be used for a variety purposes: to increase well-being, divert negative influences, and distribute the flow of *chi*. The most important stones are listed on the following pages.

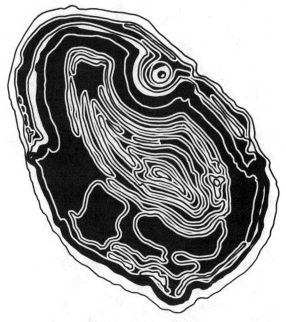

A slice of agate.

Agate

Agate provides protection, security, and certainty by stabilizing the environment against outside influences.
• *Geode:* to be displayed prominently in living rooms or bedrooms
• *Slice:* suspended or placed on a windowsill as a protection against outside influences; attached to the door of a bathroom to minimize the loss of energy.

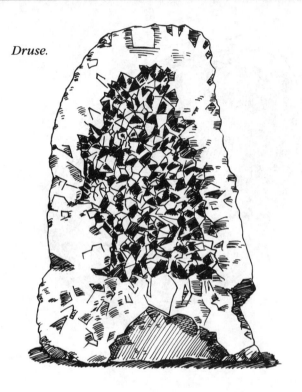

Druse.

Amethyst

The amethyst has purifying and sobering effects. It strengthens judgment and brings to light sincerity and integrity.

• *Druse:* to be displayed anywhere (should be large enough to complement the room); it cleanses the atmosphere.

• *Clusters:* to support meditation.

Cluster of crystals.

Rock Crystal

Rock crystals provide neutrality and clarity, strengthen one's own point of view, and increase the effect of other stones.
• *Crystal or cluster of crystals:* to be displayed in a room or house to bring clarity; on the desk to strengthen decision-making.
• *Pointed crystal:* in the middle of a room to strengthen its center; on a windowsill to guide the flow of energy.

Fluorite

Fluorite stimulates self-determination and helps one to remain resolute in case of injustice and oppression.
• *In clusters or individually:* on the desk to promote good study habits.

Smoky Quartz

Smoky quartz increases endurance and concentration.
• *In clusters or individually:* as a paperweight on the desk.

Rose Quartz

Rose quartz promotes openness and generosity toward oneself (love of self) and others, and strengthens empathy.
• *Unpolished stone:* as decoration on the night stand; or on the dining room or living room table to promote a sense of fellowship among visitors.

Ba Gua Area:

Semiprecious stones can be placed almost anywhere, depending on the desired effect. There are no limits—use your imagination and creativity.

Important:

To avoid unwanted side effects, make sure that a crystal or a cluster of crystals with sharp points is not pointing at a person's bed, place at the table, etc.

Cleaning Crystals:

Crystal clusters, druse, and geodes are self-contained, closed systems and clean themselves. This is why the amethyst druse is perfect for cleaning other stones. You simply put it in the middle. To remove dust, use a small brush.

Growth and retreat.

Spiral

The spiral is a widely known symbol and is closely related to the circle. Its dynamic—depending on how it is viewed—expresses concentrated power or growth, where energies move either toward the center or away from it. Like the classic labyrinth, the spiral serves as an example of the flow of life. As a motif, it is often found carved into walls, stones, and rocks in megalithic tombs. One possible explanation is that the spiral seems to have been placed in such a way that on the day of the solstice, the sun's rays touch and split the spiral exactly in half, which may be an expression of the belief in death and resurrection.

Geomancy teaches that spirals have pulsating energy fields. When used as a design in a garden, spiral shaped vegetable beds have proven to yield a better harvest than square or rectangular beds. One explanation for this might be that the whole universe, including galaxies, clouds, and oceans, moves in spiral fashion. Even on a very small scale, we see that snails and bivalves live in spiral-shaped shells.

In the West, the symbolism of the spiral is easy to understand. It is a representation of the macrocosmos here on earth.

Applications:
- As a design for a herb bed in the garden
- As a stone mosaic in front of the house to collect energy
- In the center of the house, to collect the energies of the universe.

Ba Gua Area:
Tai chi (center)

Fertility and healing.

Spring

Where trees and a spring whisper in your dream,
You are in the presence of safety and the Fountain of Youth.

—E. Aeppli

From the very beginning, people all over the world have honored the places where water emerges from the earth. A spring was considered the home of the gods, because people believed that everything godly came into being and was made visible there. Our ancestors gathered at springs in order to make contact with the other world. Christianity exchanged the gods for saints, and to this day, on certain holidays or special feasts, processions are held whose destinations are springs. Many ancient and important churches were built on top of springs or have incorporated springs within their walls.

A spring is a gift from earth; its waters revitalize, heal, and enrich. No wonder saints have appeared at springs and people make pilgrimages to them!

For the ancient Greeks, springs were honored as female goddesses, imparting creativity and healing, and were considered the symbols of eternal, never-ending life and rebirth.

Applications:
• In an indoor pond or part of an outdoor pond, as a source of energy.

Ba Gua Areas:
• Wealth
• Parents
• Career

Affirmation:
The power of the spring helps me to regenerate. Within me resides an undying spring of strength.

Harmony in matter.

Square

The square is a geometric symbol that allows people to orient themselves in a place. Unlike the circle, the square has an ordering system that also seems to be innate to human beings. As is the case with the cross, the square corresponds to our need to make sense of a random world by giving us bearings, proportions and orientation.

The phrase "squaring the circle" expresses our profound desire for finding a harmonious connection between the elements of heaven and earth (see drawing on the left of a gothic window).

Many important buildings, such as temples and palaces, were built on a square foundation. Whole towns—e.g., Peking in China and Mannheim in Germany—were designed in chessboard fashion, to make it easier to keep control over the inhabitants as well as strangers coming into or leaving the city.

In feng shui, the square is assigned to the element Earth. It stands for the earth (yang) and for the human body. The square is also considered an ideal design for homes. It provides peace, safety and stability.

Magic squares (see Magic Squares pages) are known as part of the mystical symbolism of numbers in the Far East and the West and are used in feng shui as a basis for calculations and identification.

Applications:
• Square flowerpots outside the front door to symbolize and invite peacefulness
• Inside a circle as a symbol of heaven and earth
• As a border for a mandala.

Civil servant with stag.

Stag

The stag is an important symbol. In Western culture, because of its branching antlers that periodically renew themselves, it has long been considered the symbol of rejuvenation, rebirth, and the passage of time.

In antiquity and Christian mythology, the stag was seen as protection from poisonous snakes: burned antlers were supposed to drive snakes away. Used on coats of arms, the stag symbolized greatness, power, and serenity.

In Scandinavian mythology, the antlers of the stag were associated with the crown of the universal tree, *Yggdrasil,* or said to mirror the rays of the sun.

In China, the stag is a symbol of wealth, because the word *stag* is pronounced similarly to the phrase *good income.* A picture with a civil servant accompanied by a stag means: "May fame and wealth be yours." More often, however, the stag is considered the god of long life and is thereby a symbol of longevity.

Applications:
• As a small sculpture on the desk
• As a large garden statue.

Ba Gua Areas:
• Wealth
• Parents

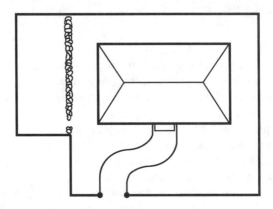

Stones

Like the mountain, the stone is a symbol of longevity. Stone rituals were practiced in many regions in China, including ceremonies in which people prayed to stones for rain. Stones were placed on street corners or in front of buildings to chase evil spirits away. Stone sculptures of lions were placed in front of government offices for the same reason.

In feng shui, stones are assigned to the element Earth, where rough stones symbolize yang and rounded, smooth stones, yin. Stones stand for calm, stability, and safety. Large stones, rocks, or a hill or mountain behind the house serves as protection. It gives the house stability, a solid character, and promises success. It is, however, important that stones or rocks are not seen as threatening and that they don't resemble evil creatures or misshapen faces.

In an outdoor pond or large indoor pond, a rock (yang) rising above the surface of the water (yin) acts as a yang balance, adding to a good yin/yang balance in the home.

As part of a garden design or displayed within a home, stones convey calm and safety and—if necessary—slow down or guide the flow of energy.

Polished floor tiles, such as granite or marble, increase the flow of *chi* and make vital energy available to the occupants of the house. They are ideal as floor coverings in bathrooms and storage rooms, but not in bedrooms.

Applications:
- To balance missing areas of irregularly shaped properties
- To contain energy, where a piece of land and the house built on it are on a slope, hill, or steep bank
- To establish harmony on a piece of land where structures are out of balance
- As large boulders on both sides of the entrance, to protect the house or provide a buffer from the land around it
- Placed indoors, as decorative symbols of quiet and safety
- As a stabilizing device in the center of the house.

Ba Gua Areas:
- Knowledge
- Marriage/Partnership
- Center

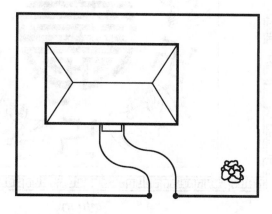

Infinity.

Swastika

The swastika (also called a *gammadion, hakenkreuz,* and some other names) consists of a cross whose ends are bent either to the left or right. It is, like the ordinary Christian cross, a symbol of return. It is the symbol for the sun and the cosmos; all of life is warmth, fire, burning, and rotation.

The legs rotating to the right means increasing energy (yang); rotation to the left means decreasing energy (yin). The swastika inside a circle symbolizes renewal.

The swastika is an ancient symbol of life that has been used for thousands of years. It is a sign of protection and healing, born from the conviction of the divine origin of life, despite its misuse by the Nazis during the 20th century.

In China, the swastika means infinity. It can be found in ornaments and decorations on clothing or walls. The picture of 5 swastikas, 5 bats, and the symbol of longevity means "luck multiplied by five and a long life" (opposite page, lower drawing).

In Buddhism, the right rotating swastika is the seal of Buddha's heart, the reason that it is often seen on the chest of a Buddha statue.

Applications:
• Together with other symbols, as wall decorations to activate the power of life in a room.

Ba Gua Area:
• Parents

The power of the gods.

Thunderbolt

In many ancient cultures, thunder is seen as a powerful and loud expression of heavenly beings—usually, gods—who are supposed to have created lightning. "Thunder is the sound of fire and the laughter of heaven" (Huang-ti Nei-ching). Thunder is also often seen as an expression of divine anger over the disruption in the order of the cosmos.

The thunderbolt (in India called *vajra,* in Tibet *dorje*) is a symbolic ritual dagger in India and Tibet. It is also known as the diamond scepter. Tantric Buddhism uses this scepter "to split ignorance down the middle to liberate understanding." It was originally the weapon of the divine Vedic god Indra, who used it to break up clouds to release rain. In Japan, the god of thunder is depicted as the red-painted god Raijin, who is surrounded by eight tambourine-type drums.

In general, thunder is considered an impressive and real expression of the power of the heavens, sometimes frightening people but also serving as a warning and protection from menacing creatures.

In feng shui, thunder is expressed in the trigram That Which Excites.

Applications:
• A sculpture of a god, on the desk, to call for order to enter
• As a talisman in the form of a thunderbolt *(dorje)*
• A drum to cleanse the air in a room.

Ba Gua Area:
• Parents

Affirmation:
The order of the universe provides me with energy and protection.

Restless and cunning.

Tiger

Originally, the tiger occupied the place of the lion as the king of the wild beasts and master of the world. It was not until later, because of the influence of Buddhism, that these attributes were given to the lion, and the symbolism of the tiger was changed.

The white tiger represents yin energy and is assigned to the underworld, which always connects the tiger to death. It is considered a messenger of the gods. In Chinese art, we find many depictions of gods, magicians, or immortal beings riding on a white tiger, because they have defeated death. The tiger is the symbol of a warrior's bravery, courage, and strength, but also his violence and destructiveness.

One of the four heavenly animals of feng shui, the tiger is asigned to the west, sunset, fall, wild storms, and turbulent winds.

In feng shui there is a saying, "Where there is a dragon there is also a tiger." The tiger is the opposite of the dragon, and is thought to be cunning, deceitful, and restless. Since the tiger side is the right side of the house or property, it is important to keep this side low-key and use lower and rounder objects or designs there. Inside the house, the right side should be kept calm and more restrained than the left side.

You don't want to give the tiger too much power and energy. As a starting point for determining the tiger's location, remember that the turtle is at the back (see pages on Four Heavenly Animals).

Applications:
• Make sure that you do not overemphasize the right side of a room. Smaller furniture would work better there.
• Outside, on the right side of the garden (right when seen from inside looking out), use soft, round, and low shapes.

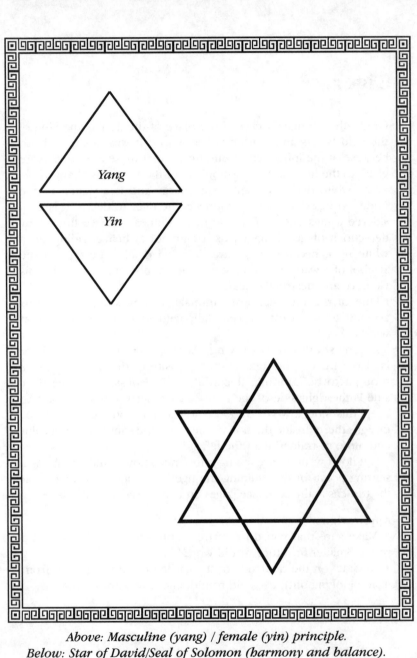

Above: Masculine (yang) / female (yin) principle.
Below: Star of David/Seal of Solomon (harmony and balance).

Triangle

The triangle is closely linked to the number three. It is the Christian symbol of the Holy Trinity (the Father, the Son, and the Holy Ghost). It was frequently seen as the Eye of God in baroque churches. Churches in the Middle Ages often had three-sided church steeples, signifying the connection between heaven and earth.

A triangle is also a well-known occult symbol, found in pyramids and obelisks. For the Pythagoreans, the triangle represented the structural principle of the universe. Later, it played an important role in witchcraft and occultism—for instance, as an amulet. Two triangles also make up the Star of David, as well as one of symbols of the Freemasons.

A triangle has different meanings, depending on the direction the tip is pointing:
• Pointing up: spirit, godly fire, masculine
• Pointing down: matter, water, female
The triangle as a symbol is often used as decoration in ceramics, where a triangle with the tip pointing down is considered a water symbol (water falling down), and with the tip pointing up a fire symbol (flames reaching up).

In feng shui, a triangle is seen as detrimental because of its irregular and incomplete shape and because of the sharp points. They are believed to be poisonous arrows that are sent into a space or room. The triangle belongs to the Fire element, as do all sharply pointed shapes. A house should never have a triangle-shaped design. If triangular shapes can't be avoided, the triangle should always be placed with the sharp point pointing up, in the direction of the life-confirming yang principle.

Application:
• As a motif in pictures or wall decorations to increase fire or yang characteristics.

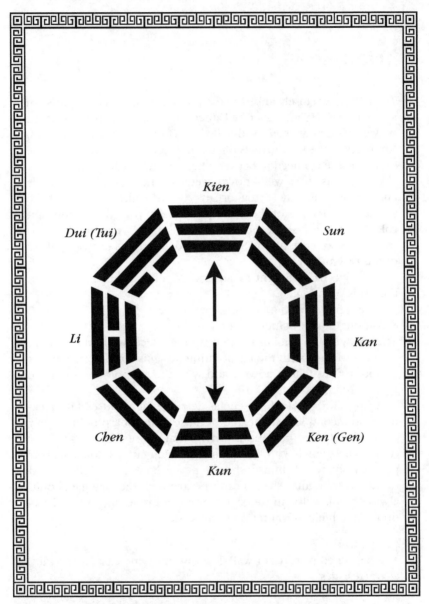

Prenatal sequence of heaven = early heaven.

Trigrams

The eight trigrams represent a further development of the broken yin lines and the unbroken yang lines. They consist of the four signs (see below) that are a representation of stillness and motion. These four signs make up the eight trigrams from which the 64 hexagrams of the *I Ching (Book of Changes)* were created by combining the 8 trigrams with each other.

Each of the eight trigrams symbolizes a power of nature and is, according to its origin, either passive (yin), or active (yang).

The oldest and best known description of the trigrams is said to have come from Fu Hsi, who placed the eight trigrams in opposite pairs in a circle, where the periphery around the circle represents time and space. This arrangement is called the "sequence of the early heaven."

The four signs:

The arrangement according to King Wen stands in contrast to the former one and represents the cosmic order. It describes the cycles and rhythms of nature, like the four seasons. This arrangement is known as the "sequence of the later heaven" or "postnatal sequence of heaven," and it is an important basis for different calculations in feng shui (see table opposite):

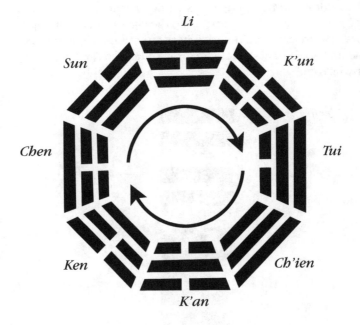

Sequence of postnatal heaven = later heaven.

Trigrams and Their Associations

Sign	Trigram	Direction	Season	Attribute	Family member
Ch'ien	Heaven	Northwest	Late fall	Creative	Father
Chen	Thunder	East	Spring	Exciting	Oldest son
K'an	Water	North	Winter	Unfathomable	Middle son
Ken	Mountain	Northeast	Early spring	Keeping still	Youngest son
K'un	Earth	Southwest	Late summer	Receptive	Mother
Sun	Wind	Southeast	Early summer	Gentle	Oldest daughter
Li	Fire	South	Summer	Clinging	Middle daughter
Tui	Lake	West	Fall	Joyous	Youngest daughter

Applications:

See pages on Trigram Band, Ba Gua Mirror, Magic Squares.

乾 CHIEN

震 CHEN

坎 K'AN

艮 KEN

坤 KUN

巽 SUN

離 LI

兌 TUI

*Cycle, rhythm,
diversity.*

248

Trigram Band

The eight trigrams correspond to the eight powers of nature. They stand symbolically for the positions of the sun during the course of the day and for the cycle of the four seasons.

Here the cycle, rhythm, flowing movement, and diversity are of primary importance, which you should keep in mind when using the band.

Applications:
• To suggest unity and change, suspended or mounted on the wall
• To break the harshness of negative energy *(sha chi)* in front of sharp corners.

Protection and long life.

Turtle

In many cultures, the turtle is a symbol of serenity, security, and protection for the back. In ancient China, people believed that the giant turtle Ao carried the earth on its back. This is why the turtle was used early on for oracles.

In countless legends, the turtle is depicted as a hero. It was to be the one who helped the first emperor tame the Yellow River in order to create fertile land. Because turtles live for so long, they became the symbol of long life, and since they seem so indestructible, they also stand for immutable order.

As one of the four heavenly animals of feng shui, the turtle of the north—the place of the strongest yang energy—represents night, winter, calm, and regeneration.

Known as the black turtle in feng shui, it stands for security, safety, and protection for the back. For an individual house to have sufficient protection, it would be ideal to have a mountain, hill, forest, or a tall building in back.

Inside the house, seating and sleeping arrangements should keep protection of the back in mind. In order to feel calm and safe, a person's head or back should ideally be protected by a wall, plant, or room divider.

Applications:
- A bed should always be placed with the headboard against a solid wall
- A desk should be placed so that the person's back is either against a wall or protected by furniture or plants
- The back of the house should be sufficiently protected. This can be achieved by building a wall or planting trees and bushes there
- A turtle paperweight in a conspicuous place near the entrance is a symbol of a long life, order, protection, and good luck.

Purity, energy, and courage.

Unicorn

The unicorn, with its white coat, a head similar to a donkey's, and a powerful horn, was considered a godlike creature possessing great energy, courage, and speed. The horn on the forehead was believed to be a magic weapon, which made the unicorn the symbol of invincibility. Legend has it that the unicorn could be captured only with great cunning and that a virgin had to be sent to where it lived. Once it saw the young maiden, it would lie down at her side, with its head in her lap, and fall asleep peacefully—making it possible for it to be captured.

This has made the unicorn the symbol of virtue. The Archangel Gabriel astride a unicorn, as depicted on many wall hangings and miniatures, became the symbol of the immaculate conception of the Christ child.

The unicorn also became the symbol of imperial justice, because the horn would destroy the guilty.

Application:
As a sculpture or picture.

Ba Gua Areas:
- Supportive Friends
- Wisdom/Knowledge
- Children

Vase

In China, a vase has the same significance as a bottle. Since the pronunciation is the same as the word *p'ing* ("peace"), it is possible to combine this symbol with many others. For instance, pine tree and plum tree branches and narcissus combined in a vase stand for "everlasting life, love, luck, and peace."

As a "treasure vase" filled with "five nourishing fruits" (grains and legumes), the vase becomes part of fertility rituals during weddings, and as a black bottle it catches spirits.

In southern China you can still find 19-inch tall (50 cm) pottery vases standing in the field. They hold the bones of relatives, which were dug up from their graves 2 years after they died. The vases are their final resting places.

Collecting good luck.

In feng shui, decorative vases are placed next to the entrance in order to invite positive *chi*, which is why these vases remain empty. These containers are usually decorated with fanciful good luck symbols, such as peacocks, birds, and peonies, or with calligraphy.

Applications:
• As decoration next to the entrance or terrace
• As a symbol of the abundance of nature, filled with flowers or plants
• As a symbol of inner emptiness and harmony, or as a decoration in the area in which you meditate (empty vase).

Ba Gua Areas:
• Knowledge
• Wealth
• Career

Affirmation:
I am a divine vessel and will always have what I need in order to grow.

Water

Water *(shui)* in the form of brooks, rivers, lakes, ponds, and oceans is a quintessential part of life. Its energies have been vital to humans since the earliest times—not only for their bodies, but also for their spirits and souls. In feng shui, water assures good fortune—particularly if a body of clean water is in view when you open the front door and when water flows in the right direction.

Every important city in the world has been built near water—not only to always have water available for food and drink, but also for transport and commerce, which is why feng shui connects water to fame and prosperity.

The quality of the water and its distance from the house is important. Water too close to the house represents danger during a flood. Water moving too fast, directly toward or away from the house, carries away too much energy too fast. Dirty or polluted water blocks the flow of *chi*.

As the original feminine energy, water is yin energy when present in lakes or calm ponds. Moving water has more yang energy; a waterfall is a good example of strong *chi*.

Effective use of water for feng shui is determined by where the water element is placed in relation to the house, whether it is a pond, fountain, well, or waterfall. According to the thousand-year Chinese calendar, a good location for a water feature in the garden at the present time (and until 2003) and for the next period (2004–2023) is in the north, southwest, east, and southeast.

If you want to include a water element in your garden, you may choose a pond, fountain, or waterfall. Let your creativity and imagination run free. Keep in mind that its size has a powerful effect on the balance. When deciding on the size, use the powerful effect of the harmony of measurements (see Measurements pages), and choose the length, width, and height of the feature accordingly. In general, rounded, oval, or circular shapes are considered positive; straight, sharp lines and corners should be avoided. The size of the water feature should be in proportion to the land and the house. If the pond or waterfall is too large, the house will look smaller and the energy of the water will overpower the energy of the house instead of nurturing it.

The water should flow gently and guide its energy toward the house. Even a small movement of water in a pond will have the desired effect.

The trigram *K'an* in feng shui means "water," symbolizing north, blue and black, night, and winter.

K'an symbolizes water.

Three Lucky Water Landscapes

Here are three good situations:

1. A wide brook with slowly moving water that flows past the front of the house, becoming narrower after passing the house.

2. Water flowing towards the house from three directions, pooling in front of the house.

3. Water hugging the house like a jade necklace in the most ideal location. A turtle, a tiger and a dragon are present on the property (see Four Heavenly Animals pages).

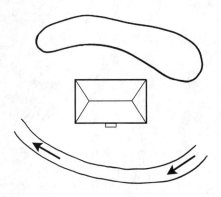

Applications:
- As a pond or small brook in the garden
- As a fountain at the entrance door to activate the flow of *chi*
- As an indoor pond or aquarium inside the house.

Ba Gua Areas:
- Wealth
- Parents
- Career

Important:
The water in the water feature must be kept clean at all times in order to support the flow of energy.

Activating and revitalizing.

Waterfall Poster

Water, one of the five feng shui elements of our planet, has great revitalizing energy. It symbolizes movement, strength, and energy. Pictures of moving water—posters of waterfalls, rivers, ocean surf, brooks, etc.—activate and invigorate the energy in a room and in our lives. A waterfall poster can influence everything: attitudes, communications, social gatherings, and the social behavior of the people in the room.

Research has shown that pictures and posters pass on information, whether people perceive the subjects in the pictures consciously or not. Depending on the subject matter, posters can raise or lower the sense of well-being, which can raise or lower the flow of *chi*—life's energy. When choosing a waterfall poster, make sure that the water is, symbolically speaking, flowing out of the poster and into the room, invigorating the energy in the room. Rivers or brooks that seem to draw the water away and make it disappear in the distance withdraw energy from a room and weaken the sense of well-being.

Choose a poster that includes trees, stones, and a lot of green to avoid activating too much water energy. Always remember that each person has different needs and therefore requires different motifs.

Since feng shui connects water with money and wealth, a waterfall poster is a favorite for supporting the flow of money.

Applications:
- To activate the flow of energy in a room
- To create vitality
- To bring water energy into the Career area
- In a conference room, a poster with gently flowing water positively influences communication.

Ba Gua Areas:
- Wealth
- Career
- Parents

Affirmation:
The vitality of water is at my disposal at all times.

Fame, honor, joy.